5.50

J979.461 Selvin, David F
S   The other San Francisco, by David F. Sel-
       vin. Drawings by Joseph Papin.   New York,
       Seabury Press [1969]
          167 p.   22cm.

       Includes bibliography.

       1. San Francisco--Hist.   I. Title.

THE OTHER
SAN FRANCISCO

THE OTHER
SAN FRANCISCO

by DAVID F. SELVIN
drawings by Joseph Papin

THE SEABURY PRESS
New York

for Nancy and Johnny
and a third yet to be chosen

Contents

1 San Francisco is...

It was a bright spring day in 1776, the year of American independence. A knot of men stood in silent awe atop the high white cliffs overlooking the narrow, cliff-ribbed strait that one day would be called the Golden Gate. "And there we saw," Padre Pedro Font wrote in his diary, "a prodigy of nature which it is not easy to describe."

A hundred years later, a flourishing city had burgeoned on the sand hills back of those cliffs. Mark Twain called it the "most cordial and sociable city in the Union." Rudyard Kipling found it a "mad city," hardly to be trusted in its vital post at the continent's "Western Gate."

"The youngest, freest, most talked-about city on earth," wrote Evelyn Wells, a newspaperwoman who chronicled many of the city's foibles. Anthony Trollope, the British novelist, doubted that he had ever visited a city "less interesting to the normal tourist." On the other hand, Novelist Frank Norris labeled it one of the few authentic "story cities" in the nation. The humorist and illustrator Gelett Burgess called it "the Impossible, the city of Miracles! . . . Earthquake and fire shall not change it, terror and suffer- ing shall not break its glad, mad spirit. Time alone can tame the town, rob it of its named charm, subdue it to the Commonplace."

William Saroyan, who spent countless hours learning the city and its people, enthused: "The wild-eyed, hard-boiled, tender-hearted, white-haired boy of the American family of cities. . . . You walk through the streets of the city and feel its loneliness and you wonder what memory is trou- bling its heart."

For nearly two hundred years, observers have tried to define San Francisco, to explain her elusive wiles. She seemed always to hold out to all comers an endless multi- tude of colors and patterns and textures; each of them chose what he liked. Her place on the tip of the peninsula, bounded by ocean and bay, crowned by hills, dimmed by fog or painted in golden light, gave her unequaled beauty. To this was added the excitement of high adventure, the tension of conflict. She wore adjectives like jewels in her crown: sophisticated, romantic, lusty, cosmopolitan. . . .

But there has always been another San Francisco.

As in the warp of a great tapestry, the threads of the other San Francisco, often unseen but only sensed, stretch back over its two hundred years: the torture of bigotry, the cruelty of fear, the hurt of exploitation; and, too, the thrust of democracy, the fever of change. Cutting across these threads is the human weft of history: the Indians; the end- lessly-mixed races, the conglomerate of nations who settled the land; not merely the adventurers and the bold but the countless silent thousands who built the city and did her unending work.

The other San Francisco lived alongside the lusty miner, the Nob Hill titan, the wealthy and the fashionable. It was a city of poor people, of working people, of black and brown and yellow people. It was a city of pain and exploitation and conflict. History paid it little attention—partly because history was made by the powerful, the rich, the stylish, and partly because this kind of history, wittingly or innocently, was color-blind.

This is the other San Francisco I have tried to define in these pages. Much of the existing record needs to be corrected, extended, filled out, and much more of the record has yet to be uncovered. But perhaps this is a start.

2 The coming of the bay

In the beginning, Eagle, Humming Bird, and Coyote stood atop a high mountain as the world around them was flooded. When the water reached their feet, Eagle carried Humming Bird and Coyote to safety on a still higher peak. In time the water went down and the world was dry. In the river Coyote found a beautiful girl and made her his wife. Their children went out over the world and they were the fathers of many tribes. Coyote told the people how to use the bow and arrow and how to kill rabbits. He told them to make mush and bread from acorns and to eat seaweed and abalones and mussels. So the world was made, according to a fragment of a Costanoan Indian legend.

Millions of years ago, the geologists have learned, the Costanoans' part—later San Francisco's part—of California lay beneath a vast sea. Water covered the land from the Farallon Islands in the west to the rugged Sierra Nevada, which the Indians called the Snowy Mountains, to the east. Weighed down by the sand and silt of centuries, strained by the hot mass of the earth's interior, the land heaved and buckled. The peaks of the Coast Range thrust up from the land. The restless ocean retreated, then, ages later, returned, rising over the coastal peaks to lap again at the foothills of the Sierra. Then the waters pulled back once more, and, with the quaking earth, scoured valleys and canyons out of the rock and sand. The once-solid land mass to the west eroded away, leaving behind the lonely rocks of the Farallones and the curving finger of Point Reyes.

On the east, massive and remote, the Sierra formed a rugged granite barrier. Its high peaks drained the water from the moisture-laden winds off the ocean. Rain and snow fed the countless streams, the creeks, the rivers that washed its slopes relentlessly on their way to the ocean below. The waters cut a canyon through the hills, gouged a channel, deeper and deeper, through the coastal peaks that lined the ocean shore. Many years later this channel was called the Golden Gate.

The land settled, the valleys dried, then the ocean returned. It pushed in through the great cut, flooding the low-lying lands behind the coastal mountains. A great bay was formed, spreading north and south some fifty miles and eastward some fourteen miles. So it was that, many thousands of years ago, San Francisco Bay was born.

Along the coast, north and south of the Gate, great forests of redwoods grew, thickest where the rains and fogs were heaviest. Chaparral blanketed the low-lying hills. Along the edges of the bay, in sloughs often choked with reeds, wading birds nested. Gulls and terns and cormorants crowded the rocks offshore. Hair seals and sea lions barked at their young playing in the tides. Fish flourished in the

ocean and rivers. Crabs and abalones, clams, shrimp, oys-
ters, mussels, clung to the rocks and along the bottom. In
the hills, small animals frequented the forests and the brush.

The prevailing winds in the summer blow off the cool Pacific toward the heated inland valleys of the continent. They
bend to the turning of the earth, striking the coast from the
northwest. The waters of the ocean, too, are deflected by
the earth's rotation. They flow in a great river, curving
southward and out to sea, pulling up great drafts of cold
water as it goes. The cold water cools the winds; the mois-
ture they carry from their Pacific journey condenses into
great banks of fog.

In early morning, gray, damp clouds of fog curl over the
coastal mountains. Sometimes the fog thrusts exploring fin-
gers through the Golden Gate, or it shrouds the entire bay,
hundreds of feet thick and stretching for miles, until the hot
summer sun burns it off. Gray, damp mornings and misty
nights alternate with days of golden sunshine. Early autumn
tends to be warmer. Winter brings the low-lying tule fogs
and the rains. A year's supply of rain, some twenty inches,
falls in the space of a few months. When the blossoms break
out in the spring, San Franciscans know that ahead are days
of sunshine, dampened often by the summer fogs, buffeted
by summer winds, but scarcely ever wet by a drop of rain.

In this land, and stretching southward to the Monterey
peninsula, lived the Costanoans. Shell mounds uncovered
around the bay suggest that their people had lived there for
perhaps some four thousand years, possibly as much as eight
thousand years. Traces of ancient man found in other parts
of California indicate even older inhabitants, who might

have migrated across a land bridge that once joined Asia and the North American continent.

In the year 1579, Sir Francis Drake's men were welcomed by Indians of the bay area. They "run very swiftly and long, and seldom go any other pace," the Englishmen noted. They admired the Indians' skill at spearfishing and with the bow and arrow. The Indians were a peaceful people, who knew little of the arts of war. Their way of living had changed only slowly, by small steps, from that of their ancient ancestors. Their world was small and they asked little of it. Neither the land nor climate nor their way of life made heavy demands on them.

Some two hundred years later, however, early visitors found the California Indian squalid and listless—"as primitive and backward as could be found anywhere on the face of the globe," one historian wrote. A French artist who visited the bay in 1816 said, "I never have seen one laugh. I have never seen one look one in the face." It seems likely that what the foreigners were actually seeing was the result of the Indians' encounter with the white man.

At the time—the latter years of the eighteenth century— some 130,000 Indians lived in California, clustered in small villages called by the Spanish *rancherias*. Neighboring the Costanoans were the Coast Miwok who made their home northward from the Golden Gate, and the Wintun who lived on San Pablo and Suisun Bays.

They lived off the land on berries, the abundance of fish in the ocean and streams, shellfish along the shores. They hunted small game and, in some parts, they relished grasshoppers, insects, snakes. They leached the bitter tannic acids from pulverized acorns to make a widely used meal. Almost nowhere in California were food crops cultivated, for the land and the waters made food abundant and the living easy.

Women wore simple aprons, made of the skin of the deer or woven from bark or reeds. They occasionally threw a wrap of deerskin around their shoulders. They took great pains with their hair, dressing it in intricate designs and ornamenting it with shells and bones and feathers. Men usually went naked and barefooted; in cold weather they used blankets of otter or deerskin and moccasins.

Home was typically a cone-shaped or domelike building, fashioned from bulrushes or reeds, sometimes plastered with bark or brush. They built large assembly houses, perhaps fifty feet in diameter, dug partway into the ground and coated with earth or brush. Some built sweathouses that were used for sweat baths—followed by a dip in a nearby pool or river—and also for treating illness. The sweathouses sometimes served, too, as a clubhouse or dormitory for the men of the village.

Many Indians became expert at making baskets which they used as cooking bowls, for storage, and in many other ways. They made whistles of bird bones, flutes of cane or elder wood, rattles from split sticks. They played a variety of games and loved to gamble on the outcome.

At night, especially in the wintertime, the Indians gathered in the assembly house to hear the legends of their people. The stories told of both great and simple things—from the creation of the world to childish or even obscene tales. Animals played important roles in their tales; Coyote who was featured in the Costanoan story of how the world was made was both hero and villain, portrayed in roles ranging from creator to trickster.

Another Indian legend told how, after the world was made, the Golden Gate was formed in one great cataclysmic stroke. The land rumbled and shook and the mountains split. The ocean rushed through in a single massive wave.

The Indians' world was simple and primitive. Nothing in it or in their way of life had prepared them for their meeting with the foreigner.

3   The dream of riches

The dream of wealth, like a powerful magnet, drew men irresistibly into the unknown. Columbus sailed to the uncharted west seeking a short route to the fabled riches of the east. Balboa, Cortez, Ulloa, Coronado, Ferrolo, Cabrillo, pursued the dream halfway around the world. In its name, they found the Pacific Ocean and conquered the Mexican subcontinent. They traveled the peninsula of Lower California, explored the American Southwest, discovered San Diego Bay, probed the California coast.

Half a century after Columbus, Spain boasted a vast, loosely held empire stretching from the Caribbean to the Philippines, from New Mexico to Cape Horn. It had been conquered, not in the name of the Spanish nation, but of the crown. Her explorers and soldiers had been accompanied wherever they went by the fathers of the Roman Catholic Church. They brought with them, too, a broad mixture of races that in time would be reflected throughout the New Spanish World. Both Europeans and Africans, pale skin, swarthy skin and black, manned the Spanish expeditions to the new world and settled in her colonies.

In sharp contrast to later conquering armies, the Spanish did not look on the Indians of these new lands merely as subjects. They were to be taught the Spanish religion and language, Spanish habits and customs. Intermarriage was not only accepted but encouraged. The native was to be integrated into the people of New Spain.

Into this New Spanish world in 1579 sailed the intrepid Captain (later Sir) Francis Drake on a freebooting tour of the world. Drake sailed up the west coast of the Americas in the *Golden Hind,* raiding Spanish settlements and Spanish ships, loading his ships with booty as he went. Then he sailed north to find a harbor where he could refit his ship and rest his men before sailing west across the Pacific.

Somewhere around the 38th parallel, he found "a faire and good Baye," his chaplain, Francis Fletcher, noted, "with a good wind to enter same." He found, too, a warm welcome from the Indians. They exchanged gifts and the Indian chief bestowed a crown of feathers on the white chief. The Indians lived in small huts along the shore. Here Drake and his men careened the *Golden Hind,* scraped her bottom, and calked her hull. After thirty-seven days, they prepared to leave. To "a great, firme post," Chaplain Fletcher recorded, Drake nailed a brass plate, taking possession of the land "in the Name of Herr Majesty Queen Elizabeth of England and Herr Successors Forever" and naming it "Nova Albion." In a corner of the plate he fastened an English sixpence bearing the Queen's likeness. They sailed then, pausing briefly at the Farallones to take seal meat aboard, then westward for England.

Some historians believed that Drake had sailed through the Golden Gate, making camp on the Marin shore of the bay. Later evidence, though, strongly argued that Drake had camped elsewhere and that San Francisco Bay itself was still undiscovered when he sailed for England.

Sebastian Rodriguez Cermeno's luck was worse. He sailed from Manila in the Philippines in 1595 carrying 130 tons of valuable cargo—silks, China ware, spices—in his ship, the *San Agustin.* He was under orders, too, to seek a safe harbor along the California coast for the Manila galleons, like his, making the annual trip to New Spain. Near the 38th parallel Cermeno found just such a port. It lay under a curved spit of land called Point Reyes, a great half-moon of a bay which Cermeno named *La Bahia de San Francisco.* Today it is called Drake's Bay and many contend it is in fact the site of Drake's visit. There Cermeno anchored, exchanged gifts with the Indians, made a journey or two inland. As his stay neared its end, a great storm drove the *San Agustin* ashore and battered it to pieces. Cermeno built a small launch, loaded aboard his men and what cargo he could rescue, and sailed southward for Mexico.

In 1602, Sebastian Vizcaino led two ships northward seeking the fabled Lake of Gold, said to yield pearls as big as hazelnuts. Far to the north Vizcaino found a port he claimed would furnish ideal anchorage for the Manila galleons. Huge forests of pine marched down to the shore; the land was well watered; water fowl and land animals were plentiful. He named it in honor of the Count of Monterey, then viceroy of New Spain. On his return, Vizcaino ardently urged colonization of California with Monterey as a base.

The rulers of New Spain, though, paid no heed. For the next century and a half, her northern empire lay baking sleepily in the sun. The viceroyalty placed little value on the country that lay beyond the Rio Grande; larger interests southward to Buenos Aires held her attention. Alta California—the northern reaches of the Spanish empire in California—seemed remote and unimportant.

Far to the north, though, the Hudson's Bay Company was pushing deeper into the wilds of Canada. It had not yet found the northwest passage it sought but it had found growing wealth in furs. At the same time Russian trappers were moving into Alaska. Among the Spanish, the Franciscan missionaries were anxious to extend the domain of the Church. And the Manila galleon still needed a safe harbor after its landfall on the west coast. The accumulating pressures finally moved Spain to action.

In 1768, Don Jose de Galvez, on behalf of the Spanish monarch, Charles III, ordered land and sea expeditions to defend and colonize Alta California. To lead them he chose Don Gaspar de Portola, a soldier born and raised on the frontier, and Fray Junipero Serra, Father President of the Franciscan missions, a tough, courageous, single-minded missionary. They were to take possession of the port of San Diego and Vizcaino's port of Monterey. Their land and sea expeditions, after harrowing journeys, joined forces at San Diego and on July 14, 1769, set out for Monterey.

Sergeant Jose Francisco Ortega, scout and pathfinder for the party, led the way with half a dozen soldiers. Portola

headed the main party, which included Fathers Crespi and
Gomez, Lieutenant Pedro Fages, Costanso the engineer,
soldiers and muleteers and an armed escort of leather-jack-
eted *soldados de cuera,* at least one of them a mulatto, Juan
Antonio Coronel. There were mulattos, too—sons of mixed
marriages in which one parent was black—among the drivers in the rear guard which, under Captain Rivera, drove
the force's spare horses and mules. Portola one day would
be California's first governor, Fages its first commandante,
Rivera his successor. Among the ranks were men bearing
names that would come to be well known in California:
Amador, Alvarado, Carillo, de Cota, and many more.

Northward they marched. They camped one night on a
tree-lined stream to observe the jubilee of Our Lady, The
Queen of the Angels of Porciuncula, whence in time came
the name of Los Angeles. They passed through an Indian
village whose inhabitants showed unusual skill at building
canoes and called it Carpinteria. A sea gull killed at the
pass where their trail turned eastward into the Santa Inez
Valley led to the name Gaviota. They climbed the rugged
mountains and then, tired, sick, exhausted, they followed
the Salinas River to a large bay, surrounded by a forest of
pines. They doubted, though, that it was the port that
Vizcaino had described.

They pushed on north. They crossed the Rio del Pajaro,
named for a giant of a bird, seven feet tip to tip, stuffed
with straw by the Indians. They passed the site of Santa
Cruz, continued up the coast past Half Moon Bay, then
halted where the Montara Mountains came down to the
sea. Next morning, they crossed Point San Pedro. For the
first time they saw the great ensenada that is known today

as the Gulf of the Farallones. Off to the left stood the rocks
of the Farallon Islands. To the north an arm of land stretched
out to sea, bordered on the right by white cliffs. It was, they
decided, Cermeno's Bahia de San Francisco; the outstretched
arm of land, Point Reyes.

Next day, Sergeant Ortega led his advance party northward to explore the coast. Meantime a party of hunters
left the camp to look for deer in the mountains to the east.
The hunters returned that night to report that a "great
estero"—an arm of the sea stretching many miles—lay on
the other side. On the third day, Sergeant Ortega returned
to report that his way had been blocked by a huge estuary
running far back into the land.

Historians argue whether the hunters or Sergeant Ortega's
party were first to sight the bay. To the sergeant, though, as
to Portola and the others, sick and half-starved, it seemed
no more than an impassable barrier to further exploration
to the north. Portola noted in his diary that "they had
found nothing." They turned back.

At San Diego, supplies were low, the men exhausted.
Portola was ready to abandon the whole project; unless the
supply ship arrived by a certain date, he was prepared to
leave. The good fathers, Serra and Crespi, though, vowed
they would stay to their last breath. They prayed for relief. Just in time, the *San Antonio* sailed into port with corn,
flour, rice. That spring, Portola reurned north, this time
accompanied by Father Serra. He was satisfied now that
the bay of pines they had passed by was, in fact, Monterey.
There, on June 3, 1770, under the shelter of a great oak,
Portola and Fathers Serra and Crespi took possession in
the name of His Majesty Don Carlos III, King of Spain.

There they established the first presidio and the second mission in California. On November 12, in that same year, Don Pedro Fages, California's first commandante, was ordered to explore the port of San Francisco and to establish there a presidio and mission. It was six months before Lieutenant Fages received the order, another year before he gathered the men and supplies to carry it out. It would be five more years before the balance of the order—the new mission and presidio—was completed.

4 "A good haven"

Late on a summer day in 1775, as the sun was setting, the packet boat *San Carlos* sailed into the Gulf of Farallones, nine days out of Monterey. Her commander, Don Juan Manuel de Ayala, was under orders to chart San Francisco Bay.

No ship had ever before ventured into the waters of the Golden Gate. Rather than risk his ship against the forbidding cliffs and a tearing tide, the lieutenant sent a party of men ahead in a small boat. They soon vanished into the gloom of evening. With night coming on, and no sign of the small boat, Lieutenant Ayala stood in through the uncharted passage, pushed along by a heavy tide. His anchor finally took hold in twenty-two fathoms, along the strait's north shore—just off what is now Sausalito.

The Indians received his advance party warmly, with food and gifts. Ayala spent a month prowling the eastern and southern reaches of the bay. On his charts a large island, not far from his first anchorage, was labeled *Isla de*

17

Los Angeles. Another, thick with pelicans, he named *Isla de Alcatraces*. Of all Ayala's names—and he labeled most of the bay's prominent features—only these two remain. In September, his work done, Ayala sailed for Monterey.

To Viceroy Bucarelli, he praised the port, "not only for the beautiful harmony that offers to the view," but for its fresh water, wood, and abundant ballast. He found the climate cold, healthful, and "free from those troublesome fogs which we had daily in Monterey." The Indians, he added, are "so constant in their good friendship and so gentle in their manners, that I received them with pleasure on board several times. . . ."

Back in Mexico, a hardy, frontier-born soldier, Juan Bautista de Anza, was trying to get royal permission to open a land route between Sonora in Mexico and Monterey. Anza's father, before him, had urged such a route. Now Anza offered to pay much of the cost, asking only for twenty or twenty-five soldiers. The answer was long delayed; the viceroy and his advisers had many questions. Finally, the possibility of new missions and of extended trade, along with strong encouragement from Father Serra —now back in Mexico City—won Viceroy Bucarelli's consent.

Anza set out in January, 1774. His small force overcame Indians, parching heat, days on end without water, the treacherous sands of the desert, and the rocky heights of the San Jacinto Mountains. They turned up—much to the surprise of its friars and soldiers—at the mission of San Gabriel. From there to Monterey was a relatively easy leap.

Anza's highly successful trip won him authority and generous support for an expedition to colonize San Francisco Bay. He was given a company of soldiers who, with their families and after a year in the service, would be given land and become settlers. Anza was authorized to recruit additional settlers in Mexico's northern provinces. Like so many of the similar companies, this was a thoroughly motley crew. Among them were Spaniards, mestizos—the children of Spanish and Indian marriages; mulattos—children of Spanish or Indian and African parents; and the Indians of Mexico. On October 23, 1775, Anza's party set out—pack mules, horses, beef cattle; muleteers, vaqueros, servants, soldiers, and 160 women and children. Father Pedro Font in infinite detail recorded the hardships of the long trail. They ran into bitter winter storms—rain, snow, and harsh, biting cold—but after seventy-three days they reached safety at San Gabriel. Soon after, they rested at Monterey. Eight babies had been born in the course of the journey.

Anza was a sick man, barely able to struggle from bed, when he reached Monterey. Still, ten days later, over his doctor's vigorous protests, he mounted horse and led a small party north. With him were Father Font and Jose Joaquin Moraga and an escort of eleven soldiers. One day, soon after, under a bright spring sun, they stood on the cliffs of the Golden Gate. Below the cliffs, at the bottom of a small slope, was a small, natural harbor. From here, Father Font wrote, the eye could reach out to the islands beyond the mouth of the port, to the ocean beyond, and to a great part of the port itself. Here Anza erected a cross to mark the site of the future presidio of San Francisco. A few miles to the south, he found a small lake formed by little streams flowing off Twin Peaks and drained by Mission Creek. Anza called it Laguna de Manantial but a priest later called it Laguna de Los Dolores, the name it gave to the mission that was built alongside.

The party marched into the hills of the East Bay, then, satisfied he could not reach the northern shore, Anza turned back to Monterey. There, he turned over his command to Lieutenant Moraga and returned to Mexico. Soon afterward, Moraga led his party of settlers north. To establish the presidio, he had a sergeant, two corporals, and ten soldiers, all—except for the commander—with their families. There were also seven families of settlers and a retinue of servants, muleteers, and vaqueros, some two hundred head of cattle and a mule train loaded with provisions and utensils. Fathers Francisco Palou and Pedro Benito Cambion, with two servants and three unmarried Indian converts, were to found the new mission. They would be met at San Francisco Bay by the *San Carlos*, sailing from Monterey with additional supplies.

The Moraga party arrived at the mission site after a ten-day march. Almost at once the "heathen of the neighboring villages," as Father Palou called them, came to visit. They brought gifts of mussels and wild seeds and they were given beads and food—"which they liked," the priest reported, "except milk which they did not wish to taste."

The settlers cut logs, explored the land, laid out sites in anticipation of building the presidio and mission. On August 10, the first child was born, the son of Ignacio and Barbara Soto. Eight days later, after beating its way against heavy winds and turbulent seas, the *San Carlos* sailed through the Gate. Work on the presidio forged rapidly

Sacramento River

nt Reyes

Drake's Bay
FARALLON
ISLANDS

GOLDEN GATE

YERBA
BUENA

SAN FRANCISCO BAY

PACIFIC

OCEAN

San Francisco
MISSION
DOLORES

SAN PEDRO
POINT

Montara

Half Moon
Bay

SAN ANDREAS

SANTA CRUZ MOUNTAINS

Guadalupe River

Coyote River

Point
Año Nuevo

SAN FRANCISCO
BAY ~ CIRCA 1776
SCALE OF MILES

8   0   8   16

Santa Cruz

Rio del Pajar.

BAY OF
MONTEREY

Salinas River

Monterey

o Carmel

ahead. On September 17, a day dedicated to Saint Francis of Assisi, patron of the new presidio, Father Palou chanted the first mass. The settlers entered the new chapel, singing *Te Deum Laudamus,* accompanied by bells and salvos of cannon, muskets, and guns that terrified the Indians. From the harbor below the white cliffs, the swivel guns of the *San Carlos* chimed in. Early in October, the Mission San Francisco de Assis was dedicated. Firearms took the place of an organ, Father Palou noted, and the smoke of muskets replaced incense. As at the dedication of the presidio, a great barbecue climaxed the celebration.

In 1768, Father Serra, given the task of establishing five missions in California, had complained that none was named for the patron of the Franciscan order. "If our seraphic father, Saint Francis of Assisi, would have his name to signalize some station of these shores," he was told, "let him show us a good haven." So, in the first year of American independence, 1776, it came to be.

5 Life at the mission

Mission Dolores was the sixth in a string of missions, finally twenty-one in all, that stretched from San Diego to the Golden Gate along El Camino Real, the King's Highway. They were intended, in keeping with traditional Spanish practice, to set the Indians on the road to Christianity (Roman Catholic) and civilization (Spanish). The Indians, in time, with education and faith, would be taken into the Church. When they were capable of managing their own affairs, they would be freed from the discipline of mission life and given a fresh start with an appropriate share of the mission's land and livestock. The missions were also, and primarily, intended to keep the Spanish crown in Alta California—all the more important because the Russians and the English were increasingly interested in the area.

To win the attention of the "pagans" or "savages," the missionary priests developed a variety of devices. Father Font noted how one of them assembled a crowd by distributing a few beads or trinkets and a little tobacco. When he had won the Indians' attention, he brought out a banner showing the Child Jesus in the Virgin Mary's arms. The natives were pleased, Father Font thought. Then the priest showed the other side of the banner—a lost soul suffering punishment—and the Indians cried out.

Small gifts, food, friendliness, and acts of kindness at first were the core of the efforts to induce the Indians to accept the Church. Little rewards and food were often enough to persuade them to lend a hand in clearing land or erecting the mission buildings. As they worked alongside the priests, they heard the stories of the Virgin Mary and the Christ child, the rewards of eternal salvation or the terrors of damnation. Food, clothing, shelter, eventually land and livestock, were held out as rewards for accepting the faith.

Serra and Palou insisted on using only spiritual arguments, along with social and economic inducements. They wanted only those who offered themselves without threats or physical compulsion. These milder methods, however, soon became inadequate. Then the priests frequently sent out parties to encourage the Indians to come to the mission. At first the expeditions were peaceful and friendly. Sometimes they were accompanied by Indians who had already accepted the mission life. Later the parties were backed by soldiers and, with increasing frequency, resistance was met with force.

The Indians' life in the mission, Captain Frederick Beechey, an early English visitor, sniffed, ought to be better than in the forests where they were obliged to run naked and depend solely on acorns for food. Here, at Mission Dolores, some eighteen hundred Indians (at the peak) lived and worked. At first there had been what Governor Fages called only an apology for a church. It was 54 feet long, built of wood, plastered with clay and roofed with tules. Adjoining was a wooden house, about 30 by 15 feet, that housed the priests. Later a new church was built; around it houses formed a rough oblong, opening on an inner square. Here were the work rooms, warehouses, houses where the neophytes—the new converts—lived. Not far off, too, was the Indian village, their conical-shaped houses formed in crude streets. Beyond the buildings were the mission gardens and pastures. It made a fair-sized village, said the artist Ludovic Choris who visited the mission in 1816 aboard the Russian ship *Rurik*, "plain and reasonably clean and well kept."

The mission Indians attended religious services morning and evening. They were taught the Lord's Prayer in Spanish, passages of the litany, how to cross themselves. Statues and pictures lined the walls of the church and the mission buildings, illustrating the religious teachings, depicting saints and angels, hell and heaven. If they persevered, the Indians were baptized. If they refused, Captain Beechey noted, they were imprisoned for a few days. Then, he said, they were allowed to walk around the mission "to observe the happy mode of life of their converted countrymen." If they still refused, they were shut up again until they were ready to accept their new faith.

Men and boys worked in the fields, cultivating crops and watching over the mission's herds. They worked at tanning and weaving, as shoemakers and bricklayers, carpenters and blacksmiths. Women carded and spun wool and wove it into cloth. They sewed and cooked. Children, too, were given

their tasks—helping with the weaving or standing guard
over ripening crops. The neophytes were taught that they
would, in time, share in the fruits of their labor, that the
land they worked and the herds they cared for would be
their own when they were capable of managing them.

To the kitchen off the large inner square each family
came for its daily rations. Breakfast and supper was usually
atole, a gruel of corn, wheat, and barley. The main meal of
the day at noon was *polzole,* a thick soup of grains, pigs'
feet, vegetables, and meat. The Indians were also supplied
raw provisions. Each family had its own small garden plot,
raising onions and garlic, melons, pumpkins, fruit trees. "It
appeared incomprehensible to me," a visitor in 1818 commented, "how anyone could consume so much nourishing
food three times a day."

There had been days, though, and they came again, when
the food was short, the supplies inadequate. The religious
leaders feuded with civil authorities; the supply ship from
Mexico was delayed or failed to appear; crops failed, sometimes from indifference and neglect.

On Sundays the mission population attended church services, the children often assisting the priests. Following services, the Indians gathered in the open area. The men
adorned themselves with feathers, ornamented girdles, and
bits of shell. They painted their bodies with lines of black,
red, and white. They danced, then, in small groups, clapping
hands, singing and striking split sticks together. Women
danced in their own small groups. Often they gambled—
tossing bits of wood at a designated spot and wagering
tools and ornaments and clothing on who threw closest.

The Indians received no pay for their labors, only their

food and housing. The men also received a blanket a year, a loin cloth and serge blouse; women, serge material for a "petticoat."

To the Indian, the Spanish purpose, however well intended, must have had little meaning. The Indian had often worked hard to wrest food and shelter from his environment—whether fishing or hunting, gathering acorns or plants, or preparing them for use. The work he knew, though, was intermittent and irregular; it came with the time and the season—when the fish were running or the acorns ripe. Then he rested or played until need required another burst of work. But regular, daily work for the mission, for a specified number of hours, often for no purpose he clearly understood, was no doubt difficult to understand. Doubly difficult was why he must work so the soldier or priest might eat.

The mission Indians seemed oppressed by their life. Choris remembered them appearing fretful and thin, "and they constantly gaze with sadness at the mountains which they can see in the distance." The reluctant were whipped to work. Often, as spring came on, they wandered away into the hills. They ran away complaining of being flogged or of hunger or of seeing friends beaten. Sometimes harsh weather drove them back; sometimes mission soldiers dragged them back. Sometimes they did not return at all. "Starvation and stripes," a historian commented, "indeed attended the perverse Indian wherever he went."

The Indians resisted, but seldom in widespread or well-organized revolt. Mission parties made up of baptized Indians, seeking converts or runaways, were sometimes attacked. One party of fourteen neophytes was ambushed and

half of them killed. Father Fermin Francisco de Lasuen instructed the priests to stop sending Christian Indians on these tasks. "The risk is too great," he said. He advised them to be content with "persuading these gentiles . . . who come and go spontaneously." The practice persisted, however. Soldiers, too, were frequently used to recapture the runaways or round up new recruits.

White settlers were few and the need for labor great. Ranchers and soldiers sometimes attempted to persuade the Indians to come to work for them; often they were simply captured and forced to work. The raids grew to what one observer called "a major industry" before the virtual slavery was finally outlawed. Though nominally free, the Indian ranch worker had scarcely more freedom than the mission Indian.

In 1821, 1,801 Indian neophytes lived at Mission Dolores. The number had been about 1,100 in the preceding decade. At the time, the mission's herds included some 11,000 head of cattle, 10,000 head of sheep, several score of mules, and nearly a thousand horses. The Mission harvested each year some five or six thousand *fanegas*—about ten or eleven thousand bushels—of wheat, barley, corn, beans, and peas. Throughout California, the twenty-one missions used the manual labor of some 30,000 Indian converts (roughly a quarter of the state's Indian population) to produce enormous quantities of grains, food, and materials, and raise great herds of livestock.

Soon after the Mexicans won their independence from Spain in the 1820's, the revolutionary government moved to liquidate the great church empire. A secularization act in 1833 ordered the mission wealth broken up, the land and

livestock distributed among the Indians. Where distribution was actually made, gambling, thievery, and sheer fraud
soon relieved the unsophisticated Indian of his share. In
many instances, no distribution was made. Some mission
Indians attempted to return to their ancestral ways of life;
some were held as serfs on the great ranchos.

Mission Dolores was among the first to be taken over.
Its buildings, lands, and livestock—valued at some $60,000
in 1835—were put in the hands of a civil administration.
Instead of being distributed among the Indians, its assets
dwindled until in a few years they were worth little more
than the mission's debts. No property was ever actually
divided among the Indians, the historian Bancroft reported.
A visitor in 1841 found some fifty of them living in hovels
around the mission, cultivating small patches of land. The
mission buildings were in ruins, no longer holding even a
resident missionary. The presidio, too, was in ruins—occupied by a sublieutenant and five families. The mission
was ordered sold at auction in 1845, but there were no
takers. It was formally restored to the Church by the
United States in 1858.

The impact of these sixty years of mission life on the
Indians was harsh and violent. It disrupted their accustomed
way of life, leaving immeasurable psychological damage in
its wake. Changes in diet led to malnutrition and epidemics
of disease. Increasingly, the clash of the incoming tide of
colonists, later the ranchers and the miners, exploded in
forced conversions, virtual slavery, brutality, violence. By
1832, the Indian population of Alta California had fallen
from an estimated 133,500 in 1770 to 98,000. But disas-
trous as these years had been, the worst was yet to come.

6   *The rancheros*

On a dark November night in 1792, Captain George Vancouver sailed His British Majesty's sloop-of-war *Discovery* into the Golden Gate. Guns boomed out in salute from the fort atop the white cliffs—*Puntil del Cantil Blanco*—and Vancouver returned the salute. Thinking he would soon come upon the lights of a town, he sailed on, but no lights appeared. He anchored in a nearby cove. At daybreak he found himself in a small bay, cattle and sheep grazing on the nearby hills. Soon a party of horsemen from the presidio rode down the slope. Over breakfast they welcomed Vancouver—the colony's first non-Spanish visitor—and offered him every accommodation.

The cove was known locally as Yerba Buena—a reference to the "good herb," a mintlike vine that grew in abundance around its sloping beach and hillsides. Governor Borica used the name in a letter in 1797 in a way that indicated the little cove was already known by the name. Its generous and protected anchorage subsequently saw a good many more visitors, but it was not until 1835 that it became the site of a small village. Meantime, the magnificence of the colony's port gained her little. Her Spanish rulers had proclaimed exclusive control over California and their representatives along the coast sought to keep—or turn—foreigners away. Foreign settlers were scarce; by 1820, few more than a dozen had become permanent residents. As the years went by, the Mexicans became engrossed in their efforts to win independence from Spanish rule, then establish their own. They grew increasingly indifferent to the needs of these remote outposts in Alta California.

The Russian ship *Juno*, though, sailed boldly into the Gate in the spring of 1806, blithely ignoring the fort until out of reach of its cannons. It anchored then, and its commander, Nikolai Rezanov, sent an emissary to identify him and his ship. He was a chamberlain of the Czar of Russia and an agent of the Russian American Fur Company based in Alaska. He said he sought supplies, but it soon became clear that he was more interested in negotiating a base for Russian fur hunters along the California coast.

He went ashore to be entertained by the family of Don Jose Arguello, commandante of the port. Almost at once, he fell in love with Don Jose's ambitious and dissatisfied daughter, Concepcion. Rezanov courted her, even while he negotiated with her father. When he sailed he carried not only a proposed treaty needing only the approval of the Czar and the King of Spain but Concepcion's promise to marry him. For years Concepcion awaited his return, but no word came. Finally she entered a convent, only to discover many years later that her fiancé had died on his way to Moscow. As the writer Bret Harte told of the romance, she learned of her beloved's death from an English traveler who inquired, unaware of Concepcion's identity, whether Rezanov's sweetheart yet lived. A hush fell over the dinner table; then from under a nun's white hood came the words softly, "Senor, pardon, she died, too."

The Russians returned a few years later; on the coast north of the Golden Gate they established the base Rezanov had sought and called it Fort Ross. The fur-hunting fell off, though; efforts to develop an agricultural center failed. The cool reception by the Spanish discouraged the Russians even more. They sold the land and left the country.

In the meantime, a new way of life was developing in Alta California. At its core were the great land-grant ranchos and their rancheros—the new Californians. The land grants were both a reward of a grateful government as well as an incentive to settle (and hold) the land. Both the Spanish and, later, the Mexican governments handed out generous grants to soldiers and others who had served in the Anza and Portola expeditions, who had manned the presidios or who had served in some special way—and to their sons and daughters, too. When the mission estates were broken up in the 1830's, many more millions of acres of California land were handed out to the favored ones. The land grants were peopled by a colorful array of racial stocks. As we have read, the Spanish-speaking colonists had brought to the new world both European and African stocks and mixtures of them. These were further mingled with the Indians of Mexico and of California, and with the occasional American or Englishman who came to visit, stayed to marry an attractive daughter of one of the old families and settle down.

The new Mexican government opened California's ports to foreign vessels. The rancheros soon developed a vigorous and wealthy trade in hides and tallow. The missions had raised great herds of livestock and produce, but much of it went to sustain the mission population, the soldiers of the presidios and the representatives of their rulers. The rancheros invaded the trade, then took it over in large part after the missions were secularized. Yerba Buena became an important center of the trade.

Traders anchored in the bay, sent small boats to collect the hides and tallow. The ranchers and their ladies hurried to the ship to choose from the varied stocks of food, clothing, furniture, manufactured articles of every kind, jewelry and such, that were laid out by the traders. Russian fur trappers, whalers from many lands, as well as the hide ships, dropped anchor in the bay. Soon, fur trappers, both English and American, found their way to the coast from the Rockies a thousand miles to the east.

The newfound wealth of the ranchers displayed itself in gaudy dress. Gold and silver decorated their deerskin shoes. Their velvet or satin breeches, gold-braided and silver-buttoned, were slashed and flared at the knees. They wore wide, flat-topped sombreros, gay with gold or silver cord. Their horses, too, were smart and dashing in colorful harness, all gold and silver and shining leather.

The ranchers lived an open and hospitable life. Weddings, births, political changes, religious holidays; almost any happening was reason for a gala celebration. Horses and carriages from neighboring ranches for miles around crowded the host's ranchyard. Guests ate and drank and danced, often for days at a time. The new Californians hunted grizzly bear—as a pastime but also to protect their cattle herds. Rodeos also combined business and sport. Bull and bear fights provided a grim and bloody entertainment. The ranchers' houses were never closed; travelers were welcomed warmly with food, lodging, fresh horses. Every offer of pay was turned aside.

Many had their own companies of Indian retainers who performed the manual work of the ranch. Indian women worked as domestic servants. Mexicans and Spaniards were paid $3 to $10 a month and board for tasks requiring greater skills; the Indians were paid little or nothing. Though nominally free, the Indians were often held in virtual bondage. They could not leave if they owed the rancher money or without a written discharge attesting that they owed no debts. These formalities were easily overlooked or withheld.

Mexican rule replaced the Spanish but distance and internal problems created a growing indifference to the faraway outpost of Alta California. The rise of foreign trade sent word of the new land tumbling around the world, to New England and China, to England and Moscow. Separation of Alta California from the parent land soon became an ambition among some of her settlers, then a developing fact. The Americans made it a reality.

7   The coming of the Americans

In December, 1835, after battling heavy gales for some twenty days, the brig *Alert* "floated into the vast solitude of the Bay of San Francisco. All around," young Richard Henry Dana recalled in *Two Years Before the Mast*, "was the stillness of nature." The *Alert* dropped anchor in a little "bight" where trading ships anchored. One vessel, a Russian brig taking on supplies for Sitka, lay nearby. The anchorage lay between a small island and a cove—a gravel beach flanked by two small projecting points of land. Both the island and cove were called Yerba Buena. Westward, Dana remembered only dreary sand hills, a little grass, a few trees and, beyond, higher hills, steep and barren. Off to the northwest lay a "ruinous Presidio," and, a few miles to the southwest, the nearly deserted mission in almost as bad a state. On shore, almost the only sign of human habitation was "a shanty of rough boards put up by a man named Richardson, who was doing a little trading between the vessels and the Indians."

Dana—then a twenty-year-old who had left Harvard College to sail as an ordinary seaman on the hide ships—predicted: "If California ever becomes a prosperous country, this bay will be the center of its prosperity." As a successful lawyer nearly a quarter of a century later, he returned to San Francisco to see his prediction fulfilled.

In 1835, though, the five missions in the vicinity held no more than two hundred white inhabitants. The ranchos, stretching for miles, were widely separated. Only an occasional trader or whaler kept the port active.

The rough shanty that Dana had seen was, the records show, San Francisco's second building, other than those of the mission and presidio. The first had been four redwood posts, topped by a ship's sail, thrown up by the same "enterprising Yankee." His name was William A. Richardson and he had arrived in California in 1822 under somewhat clouded circumstances; he was either booted off the ship on which he arrived or he simply deserted.

Richardson persuaded Mexican authorities to allow him to stay in return for teaching carpentry and navigation to their young ones. He adopted Mexican citizenship and the Catholic faith and married into a California family. Governor Figueroa made Richardson harbor master of Yerba Buena and suggested he draw a plan of the town. He drew a base line—a broad street called *Calle de la Fundacion,* about where Grant Avenue runs today. At its north end it joined the westerly trail leading from the cove to the presidio; on the south it linked with the trail to the mission. Richardson's shack lay along his "foundation" street. He soon tore it down and erected an adobe house which he called *Casa Grande.* Richardson was Yerba Buena's "first" citizen in countless ways: he built its first building, owned its first lot, was its first harbor master, was involved in its first real estate transaction. Later he became owner of Rancho Saucelito in Marin county where a small bay now bears his name.

In 1836, Jacob Primer Leese sailed into the cove aboard the barque *Don Quixote*. He was an Ohioan who had been living in Los Angeles, reputed at the time as "the noted abode of the lowest drunkards and gamblers of the country." Then a little, disreputable village, Los Angeles had been settled in 1781 by a small party of poverty-stricken *pobladores*—two of them Spanish, the rest Indian, black, and mixtures of these stocks. It was, when Leese left it, the largest pueblo in California, but that said little for it. Monterey was smaller and less influential. San Francisco, a historian observed, "was little more than an abandoned mission, a decayed presidio and a cluster of adobe huts."

Leese brought with him to Yerba Buena a $12,000 stock of merchandise and enough lumber to build a house. He hurriedly ran up his house, which was also part store, next door to Richardson's. It was near enough finished for him and his neighbor to join in a great, exuberant celebration of the Fourth of July. With the Stars and Stripes flying alongside the Mexican flag, they played host to "all the beauty, wealth and fashion of California." A six-piece orchestra furnished music, accompanied by the "emphatic roar" of two small six-pounders. Their guests from miles around dined and danced and drank through the night into the next day. "Our Fourth ended," Leese wrote in his diary, "on the fifth." A few days later he landed his merchandise and reported a "brisk" trade at "satisfactory" prices.

Soon after, Leese and Richardson were joined by Nathan Spear, a native of Boston. He planted a ship's house, about 12 by 18 feet, nearby, calling it Kent Hall. Later he built a store building just to the north. In 1839, Spear welcomed his nephew, William Heath Davis. It was actually Davis's second visit; he had been there first in 1833 as an eleven-year-old cabin boy on the bark *Volunteer.* Then he remembered seeing only one person living at Yerba Buena— a Mexican named Candelario Miramontes who raised potatoes on a small patch of land near what later became the Plaza. This time he returned on the *Alert,* the hide drogher that had carried Dana back to Harvard.

That summer—June, 1839—the brigantine *Clementine* landed John A. Sutter and his party. Sutter was a Swiss immigrant who had wandered in recent years from New York to Oregon, to Hawaii and Alaska, and now to California. He obtained a grant of 50,000 acres lying near the junction of the American and Sacramento rivers, in the heart of the great central valley. There, Sutter established a fort. He gathered a motley force of sailors, Kanakas—natives of the Sandwich Islands, later called Hawaii—Mexican cowboys, and friendly Indians. Sutter planted hundreds of acres, built houses, stables, granaries, workshops. He manned and armed the fort in a style befitting the "lord of the marches of Sacramento."

William A. Leidesdorff sailed into port in 1841 as master of the schooner *Julia Ann.* He was fleeing an unhappy love affair, ruptured when he revealed that his mother was a West Indian black, his father a wandering Dane. He built the City Hotel, planted a warehouse just off the beach, built himself a cottage on the outskirts of the village. He also constructed the town's first wharf. Leidesdorff served as American vice consul, later as the town's first regularly elected *alcalde,* or mayor, a member of the town council and of the school committee. He also imported the *Sitka,* the first steamship to sail the bay. It took her six days and seven hours to make her first trip to Sacramento and proved so "cranky" to handle that—the story goes—the ship was leveled by passing the baby of one of the passengers, a Mrs. Gregson, from starboard to larboard.

Yerba Buena, though, remained no more than a small, unimportant trading village. By 1840, the presidio was useless, manned only by a handful of ragged troops, its guns rusted, ammunition scarce. World powers, though, eyed the province with interest. British and French as well as American warships were stationed on the coast, each keeping watch on the others.

Californians talked of breaking away from Mexican rule. In the states, the idea of joining California to the United States was increasingly discussed. As early as 1837, societies were being formed in the American states to emigrate to Oregon and California. In 1841, John Bidwell's company made the first overland trek. The party had expected to float down to the Pacific on rivers that rose in the Rockies; the waterless desert and the rugged Sierra came as an unpleasant shock. But other emigrant parties followed. Some settled at New Helvetia with Captain Sutter. Others made their way to Dr. John Marsh's ranch at the foot of Mt. Diablo in the East Bay. The Mexican government attempted futilely to restrict the rising flood of immigrants but was generally ignored.

President Andrew Jackson offered Mexico $500,000 for San Francisco Bay and the northern part of the province. Other presidents raised the offer to as much as 40 million

dollars. Mexico was not interested. Lieutenant William A. Slocum explored the coast for information that would be "interesting or useful to the United States." Lieutenant Charles Wilkes led a party to gather information on economic, political, and social conditions in California. Yerba Buena did not impress him but he thought the harbor was the greatest natural harbor in the world. In 1842, Commodore Thomas Ap Catesby Jones, thinking war had broken out between Mexico and the United States, sailed into Monterey and landed a detachment of troops. It promptly seized the presidio and ran up the American flag. The commodore pulled it down the next day and retired in embarrassment when he learned there was no war.

In 1843, John C. Fremont headed a second American exploring party. Fremont was a man of many talents. In his lifetime, he served as an explorer, soldier, writer, senator, first presidential candidate of the newborn Republican party. His expedition ranged the state from Lake Tahoe and Carson's Pass to the Mojave Desert. Almost before he reported to Washington, he was planning a second trip. He returned in 1845, crossing the Sierra to Sutter's Fort, continuing on to Monterey to visit Thomas O. Larkin, the American consul. For a few days, it appeared as if he were inviting an attack by Mexican forces. Then suddenly he withdrew and marched northward. Near Klamath Lake, he was overtaken by Lieutenant Archibald Gillespie, carrying urgent messages whose contents are still not fully known. Fremont said they were messages from his father-in-law, U.S. Senator Thomas H. Benton of Missouri. But his actions suggested that he was thereafter an agent of the American government. In any case, he turned back to Sutter's Fort.

Encouraged, perhaps, by the presence of Fremont's force,

a group of American settlers chose that moment to revolt against Mexican rule. They claimed the Mexicans were stirring up the Indians against them and preparing to drive them from the valley. They devised a crude flag, bearing the figure of a grizzly bear, a five-pointed star, and a strip of red flannel on the lower edge of a white cotton field. It bore the words "California Republic" in red capital letters. Early in June, 1846, under their new banner, they marched on Sonoma where they took into custody General Mariano Vallejo. Though a Mexican, Vallejo, ironically, was a firm advocate of American acquisition. William B. Ide, chief of the Bears, proclaimed their intention to establish a republican government. Said one of the men as they ran the new Bear Flag up the pole, "We have taken upon ourselves a damned big contract."

Unknown to either the Bears or to the Mexican authorities, the United States and Mexico were already at war. Hostilities had broken out in April, 1846, over the American annexation of Texas. Back of the dispute, though, had been growing pressures not only for the annexation of Texas but also for the purchase of New Mexico, the conquest of California, and the opening of new land to cotton and slavery. The war ended in February, 1848, after General Winfield Scott, "Old Fuss and Feathers," had invaded Mexico. The Treaty of Guadalupe Hidalgo ceded the disputed Texas territory to the United States and, for a small price, the New Mexico country and California. California's place in the Union, meanwhile, had been carved out first in the Wilmot Proviso which banned slavery in territory acquired from Mexico. It was confirmed in 1850 when California was, in fact, admitted as a free state, closed to slavery.

Meantime, on July 7, 1846, Commodore John D. Sloat

had landed bluejackets and marines at Monterey, had raised the American flag and proclaimed California part of the United States. Not a shot was fired. Next day, under Sloat's orders, Captain John B. Montgomery of the U.S.S. *Portsmouth* put ashore at Yerba Buena a landing party of seventy sailors and marines. Smart in white frocks, blue pants, black hats and shoes, led by a fife whistling "Yankee Doodle" and a lone drummer, the contingent marched to the Plaza. Some thirty citizens gathered to watch as a quartermaster raised the Stars and Stripes.

"Something was about to be done," a petty officer recalled, "that could not easily be undone." The *Portsmouth's* guns thundered a salute. The ship's company hurrahed, the petty officer remembered; Californians "viva-ed," "Dutchmen" cheered, dogs barked, jackasses brayed. The citizens then repaired to nearby saloons. The noise of their revelry mounted through the day until sundown when the commander sent word that the town was under martial law and "the orgies" must cease.

Captain Montgomery appointed Lieutenant Washington A. Bartlett the town's first *alcalde* under American rule. When the lieutenant heard of plans for a new seaport and commercial city called Francesca to be built on Carquinez Strait, he promptly proclaimed that the town's name henceforth—and for the first time—would be San Francisco. The name, Yerba Buena, he said, was purely local, adopted from the little cove. The new name would prevent "confusion and mistakes" and "the town would have the advantage of the name given on the public maps."

8   Interlude

On July 31, 1846, some three weeks after the Americans had taken over, the *Brooklyn* sailed through the Golden Gate. She was crammed with farmer's tools, two flour mills, a printing press, and 238 men, women, and children. Most of all, she carried Sam Brannan. In little time Brannan became a major figure in San Francisco. He performed the first marriage and preached the first sermon under American rule. He arranged the city's first jury trial, established her first newspaper. He acquired great stretches of real estate, played an important part in the city's affairs, made and lost several fortunes.

Brannan was the son of a Maine farmer. He became a Mormon missionary when he was twenty-three, commissioned by Joseph Smith, prophet and founder of the Church. Brannan chartered the *Brooklyn* after the people of Nauvoo, Illinois, scandalized by the Mormons' practice of polygamy, drove them from their midst. He loaded her with Mormon families and the goods they needed to set up a refuge in the

West. In San Francisco, "Filings," pseudonym of the petty officer who had chronicled the American seizure, reported a vague apprehension that these Mormons were "a wild, desperate people" who would soon cause trouble. But Brannan and some of his party took part in religious services on the deck of the *Portsmouth* and lunched afterward with Captain Montgomery and his officers. They left, "Filings" reported, "a favorable impression among the hearty tars."

In March, 1847, the ship *Thomas H. Perkins* landed the first detachment of the 7th New York Volunteers, under Colonel Jonathan Logan Stevenson. The men had enlisted for the duration of the war with Mexico. When peace disbanded the regiment, its soldiers would settle in California. Some of the men ended in jail and a few on the gallows. A large number attained positions of wealth and influence. Among them were bankers, the first editor of the newspaper *Alta California,* a lumber manufacturer, several members of California's first constitutional convention, and twelve members of the Russ family who found prominent places in the city's business.

In the first year under the American flag, the little town's population doubled. The *Californian* in June, 1847, counted a white population of 375. Most of it—228—had been born in the United States. Native Californians numbered thirty-eight; two had been born in other Mexican provinces. Germany contributed twenty-seven, England twenty-two, Ireland and Scotland fourteen each. There were also thirty-four Indians "of different ages," forty Sandwich Islanders, ten "Negroes." Four were born at sea. Four-fifths of the town's population were under forty years old. Two-thirds claimed they could read and write.

Among the townspeople were twenty-six carpenters, thirteen clerks, six printers, five grocers, four shoemakers, four tailors, six inland navigators. There was one schoolteacher but no school, a minister, a doctor, a lawyer. The town boasted eight stores, seven groceries, three butcher shops, three bakeries, two printing offices. It had one windmill, one apothecary shop, two blacksmith shops, and one gunsmith. The energetic newspaper counted seventy-nine buildings: twenty-two shanties, thirty-one farmhouses, twenty-six adobe buildings. In the next five months, seventy-eight new buildings were erected.

The little town huddled around the cove, flanked on the north by a rocky spur called Clark's Point. It was named for William Squire Clark who owned it in 1846. Passengers off ships lying in the cove, where the waters ran shallow, were landed at Clark's Point. They walked west on Broadway, turned to the south, crossing a bridge over Laguna Saluda, a small inlet from the bay, to reach Montgomery Street and the heart of town. On the south, the cove was marked by Rincon Point.

In 1839, Jean Jacques Vioget, a Swiss sailor and surveyor who had played the fiddle at Richardson's and Leese's gala Fourth of July party, had been hired to survey Yerba Buena. Lots in the little town had been sold or granted by the Mexican governors. These were marked on Vioget's map which hung in Bob Ridley's saloon. Names of the lot owners were simply written on the map. When it became excessively soiled, another was made and the original deposited in Ridley's safe. On Vioget's map, Montgomery Street lay closest to the bay, extending north and south from near Sacramento Street to the base of Telegraph Hill. Immediately to the

VIEW OF SAN FRANCISCO FORMERLY YERBA BUENA, IN 1846-7

west was Kearny Street, forming the southern edge of the
Plaza, later called Portsmouth Square. Just as it is today,
the Square was flanked on the south by Clay Street and on
the north by Washington.

The Americans, both informally and by treaty, assured
landholders that their Mexican land grants and titles would
be respected. American practice as it developed, though,
put the burden of proof on the landholders. The result was

long and costly litigation, a protracted period of confusion in California land titles, and a field day for fraudulent and forged claims. In the end, most of the grant holders lost the bulk of their property.

Soon after the American takeover, Jasper O'Farrell—a civil engineer who had reached Yerba Buena in 1843—revised Vioget's map. He kept Vioget's plan of square blocks, with streets intersecting each other at precise right angles, marching up and down hill without the slightest regard for topography. O'Farrell, though, slashed a great broad thoroughfare diagonally across the town, from the bay to the foot of Twin Peaks. He called it Market Street. Paralleling its southern side he imposed a new checkerboard. Landowners became so agitated with O'Farrell's changes that an indignation meeting led to a demand for O'Farrell's neck. The engineer beat a hasty retreat by boat and horse; he remained some time in Sonoma before he considered it prudent to return to the city.

On July 4, 1847, first under the American flag, the frigate *Congress* fired a national salute at midday and was answered by a big Spanish gun mounted on shore. A "large collection of ladies and gentlemen" gathered at Brown's hotel to hear a reading of the Declaration of Independence and appropriate speeches. Toasts were drunk, songs sung, and more speeches made at Portsmouth House. A ball capped the celebration.

This was San Francisco, then—a small, restless crossroads, a traders' outpost, distant, isolated. Then one day in 1848, Sam Brannan dashed excitedly down the street, brandishing a small bottle and crying, "Gold! Gold! GOLD!"

9   *The gold seekers*

The Indians lived out their time in California ignorant of gold. The Spanish found none; they stayed on the coast, disdaining what wealth the valleys and mountains to the east may have held. The Mexicans and *Californios* found wealth in hides and tallow and in the great herds of cattle that roamed over their lands. The discovery of gold fell, finally, to a moody and eccentric carpenter by the name of James Wilson Marshall.

In partnership with John A. Sutter, Marshall was building a sawmill on the American River at a place the Indians called "Culuma." Near the end of January, 1848, Marshall turned loose the water behind the mill dam to clear the tailrace. Next morning, he saw glittering particles lodged in the bottom of the channel. He told Sutter later that he hesitated to pick them up. Once he did, though, he quickly collected all he could find in the top of his hat. "Boys," he shouted to the men working on the mill, "I believe I've found a gold mine."

He tested the specks by the few simple tests he knew.

After several mornings, he headed for Sutter's Fort and demanded a private audience with Sutter. Sutter's first reaction, he said later, was to make sure his rifle was in its proper place. When Marshall told him he had dicovered gold, Sutter said he thought something had touched Marshall's brain. Then Marshall dumped his little poke of dust on the table. The two men weighed and bit and measured the dust. They tried acid on it. They consulted the *American Encyclopedia*. Finally they were convinced. Sutter returned to the mill with Marshall for a final assurance. The two men urged the workers to keep working on the mill; meantime, hoping to keep their find secret, they moved to take full advantage of it.

Sutter obtained a lease from the Indians. He dispatched a rider, pledged to secrecy, to Monterey to have the lease validated. (Governor Mason refused to confirm it, asserting that the United States did not recognize the right of Indians to lease the land.) To outdo another man's boast, the rider bragged of the discovery. A teamster delivering supplies to the mill brought back some dust and paid for a bottle of whiskey with it at Sam Brannan's store. An employee at the mill wrote some friends; they visited the mill, turned up nuggets with their knives. Returning to Sutter's flour mill at Natomo, they prospected other sites. Sutter himself talked of the discovery with several friends. He wrote about it to General Vallejo.

Slowly at first, then in growing numbers, the men at the Fort and on nearby ranches left their work to search for gold. Sutter's flour mill was left uncompleted. Tanners quit, leaving behind stacks of rotting hides. Sutter managed to get in his wheat crop but had no one to thrash it. His workmen disappeared into the hills; his once-baronial estate was soon thronged with strangers on their way to the diggings.

San Francisco's newspapers picked up word of the discovery. They were cautious if not downright doubtful. The *Californian* reported the find, but shrugged, "Gold has been found in every part of the country." E. C. Kemble, editor of the *California Star,* reported gold was an "article of traffic" at New Helvetia, but he thought plowing and planting were more urgent. In mid-April he took off on a tour of the gold country. He brought back an excited tourist's report: "See it now. Full-flowing streams, mighty timber, large crops, luxuriant clover, fragrant flowers, gold and silver."

Brannan returned to San Francisco about that time, waving his hat and displaying a bottle of gold dust. A reporter noted little knots of men, gathered on a street corner to listen eagerly to the tales of some newly arrived digger. Mild interest flared into bright excitement. San Franciscans departed for the gold fields in increasing numbers—by sloop and lighter, on horseback and afoot. By June the town was half-empty and soon virtually deserted. Businesses slammed their doors. Real estate went begging. Mourned the *Star*: ". . . as if a curse had arrested our onward course of enterprise, everything wears a desolate and sombre look, everything is dull, monotonous, dead." And the *Californian*: ". . . the field is left half-planted, the house half-built, and everything neglected but the manufacture of shovels and pickaxes." Soon editors and their crews, too, left for the gold fields.

A ship flying the Peruvian flag anchored off Yerba Buena cove. No small boats met her, no one could be seen on the beach. The captain went ashore, walked the streets for some distance before he found someone who could explain the silent town. Sailors on ships coming into the bay were granted —or they took—shore leave and headed for the diggings. Some crews simply lowered the boats and rowed off upriver. As often as not, their captains went with them. Governor Mason complained angrily that his soldiers were deserting and that gold seekers were not making proper provisions for their dependents whom they left behind.

Word spread in ever-widening circles. A ship carried it to Honolulu; the local newspaper reported the discovery of gold on page six. Hudson's Bay men carried the report to the northwest coast. Soon, two-thirds of Oregon's able-bodied men—including one who became California's first elected governor—had gone south to dig for gold. Mexico got the news and miners from Sonora flocked north, giving the name of their province to the southern diggings' most important town. Soon the gold hunters began to pour in from the Sandwich Islands, Peru, Chile. China, reported one historian, sent "thousands of thrifty wandering children, feeble, indeed, both in body and mind, but persevering, and from their union into laboring companies, capable of great feats."

In December, President Polk reported the discovery to Congress. A tea caddy carrying 230 ounces of virgin gold went on display at the War Office. Governor Mason reported to Washington that there was enough gold in the country drained by the Sacramento and San Joaquin rivers to "pay the cost of the present war with Mexico a hundred times over." (Later, he said "five hundred times" was "nearer the mark.") "Any reports that may reach you of the vast quantities of gold in California," he told the adjutant general of the Army, "can scarcely be too exaggerated for belief." President Polk relied on Mason's eyewitness report to verify the "extraordinary" accounts that otherwise "would scarcely command belief."

"Lies raced along the Atlantic seaboard," the English writer, Thomas De Quincey, reported. A million dollars a day, said liar No. 1. Don't believe it, said liar No. 2. It never exceeded half a million—and even that on no more than nine days out of ten. Even so, said liar No. 3, that's not so bad when shared among so few men.

Gold fever took on worldwide proportions. Men from all parts and of every kind set out for the gold regions. Editors and ministers joined the throng, according to historian Bancroft, and so did "the trader . . . the toiling farmer, whose mortgage loomed above the growing family, the briefless lawyer, the starving student, the quack, the idler, the harlot, the gambler, the hen-pecked husband, the disgraced, with," he conceded, "many earnest, enterprising, honest men and devoted women."

They came by sea. Some made the long—17,000 miles, four to eight months—and monotonous voyage around stormy and treacherous Cape Horn. Others cut it short by crossing Panama or Nicaragua, then taking ship again from the west coast of Central America. By happy coincidence, the Pacific Mail steamer *California* inaugurated a new steamer service from the west coast of South America in the winter of 1848–49. When she reached Panama on her maiden voyage, she found more than seven hundred gold hunters seeking passage to San Francisco. She was rated to carry 250 passengers and she already had aboard some 69 Peruvians. By a process described as "priority, lottery, bribery, trickery, and ticket scalping," accompanied by mass meetings and protest committees, she packed some 300 additional passengers aboard.

The *California* sailed into San Francisco Bay on February 28. Her passengers saw only a haphazard collection of adobe houses, wooden shacks, and tents set on a sandy hillside. For their part, the San Franciscans, clustered on hilltops and wharves, gave the ship "cheer after cheer," the *Alta California* reported; warships in the bay thundered their welcome. Passengers quickly disembarked, speeding for the gold country. On their heels went the *California's* crew, leaving behind only the captain and an engine-room boy.

Other Pacific Mail steamers followed closely behind, top-heavy with hundreds more gold seekers. At the same time, ships were arriving from all parts of the world—some six hundred by November, 1849. The larger part of them were abandoned, left swinging on their anchor chains as their crews hastily departed for the gold fields.

That spring, too, overland parties clustered impatiently at jump-off points in Missouri and Kansas, waiting for grass to spring up green and bright along the trail. Long trains of wagons, their white covers gleaming under a summer sun, were soon rumbling slowly along, a multitude of horsemen prancing alongside, companies of men traveling on foot. "Although the scene was not a gorgeous one," an eyewitness remembered, "yet the display of banners from the many wagons, and the multitude of armed men looked as if a mighty army was on its march." Their campfires at night, said another, resembled the lights of a great city.

The first parties made their way into Sacramento Valley

in midsummer: "gaunt, hollow-eyed men and women leading or carrying children," a historian described them. Behind them, thousands more battled the trail. Grass was soon
exhausted. Cholera ravaged many of the parties, then gave
way to mountain fever, finally to the tortures of the alkali
desert. Broken-down wagons, abandoned equipment, the
carcasses of thousands of cattle and horses and oxen, lined
the trail. Hastily dug graves and rude monuments counted
the death toll.

On they came: "Women, whose husbands died of cholera," a historian recorded, ". . . whole families, men,
women and children on foot, without food. Men scarcely
able to walk, who said that for two hundred miles back they
had eaten nothing but dead mules."

Rains came early that year and snows quickly mounted.
Soldiers were hurried into the valley to help the thousands
on the trail. Relief stations were set up and parties sent in
all directions with food and water, beef cattle and work
oxen. From San Francisco and the gold country came money
and supplies to finance the relief.

At the end of the trail was the hard life of a miner—"the
hardest work," one said, ungrammatically but emphatically,
"to get hold of it that you have ever saw." A man worked in
90 to 100 degree temperatures, slogging about in icy mountain streams, picking and shoveling tons of dirt and gravel.
He worked long hours with poor and often makeshift tools,
with no assurance of security or reward. He lived and
worked alone, existing on his own often bad cooking and a
limited diet. He was a frequent victim of disease, compelled
to doctor himself with what patent medicines he could lay
his hands on. Sundays were put aside for washing clothes or

a trip to the nearest camp for supplies. Sometimes there was church or what entertainment the neighborhood offered— horse racing, foot racing, dog fights, gambling, cards.

The tens of thousands working the streams and the hills brought into being a new and crude society. They were beyond the reach of formal law, but they quickly shaped their own to the strange circumstances of the gold country. Basically, the miners agreed, a man was entitled to claim and hold a piece of land that he could reasonably work by himself. As long as he did no harm to others, he was free to do pretty much as he chose. Men who broke the rules were brought before a miners' meeting. A judge was elected, a jury chosen, counsel appointed. Witnesses were heard and judgment rendered. The guilty were flogged, banished from the camp, or in some cases hanged.

The tremendous outpouring of gold from the Sierra foothills sent tremors around the world. It spurred new industry and business, stimulated agriculture and transportation, sent its shock waves into lands thousands of miles distant. It set in motion the inexorable forces that soon ended California's isolation and tied her inextricably to the United States.

The tidal wave of gold seekers laid waste the Indians' way of life. It overran their lands, drove out and killed the game, muddied the rivers, chopped down forests. It ignored Indian claims to the land and met their resistance with murder—both as public policy and private practice. Survivors fell victim to disease and starvation or were simply confined to reservations.

The Spanish dream of integrating the Indian and Mexican people into the social and economic life of the land was trampled into the dust. The Mexicans and other Latins were tolerated but seldom fully accepted. Chinese, oddities at first, were increasingly victimized by harassment and discrimination, by both mob and individual violence. Attitudes of the dominant Anglo-American influence ranged, in the summing-up of John W. Caughey, "from a thoroughly democratic willingness to accept individuals on the basis of ability . . . through amusement at outlandish practices, to indifference, condescension, discrimination, and cruelty."

Paralleling these attitudes was another: the old distinctions of wealth and education and class—at least as they applied to white men—were largely abandoned. No man worked for wages. Every man was expected to live by the sweat of his own labor. Doctors and lawyers worked and lived in the gold camps on equal terms with illiterate laborers and uneducated farmers. It was a democracy of hard work. "Labor is honorable," Senator David Broderick told the United States Senate. ". . . no station is so high and no position so great that its occupant is not proud to boast that he has labored with his own hands. There is no state in the union, no place on earth, where labor is so honored and well rewarded."

So this unique experience in the gold fields was added to the developing amalgam of cultures and civilizations that became the hallmark of San Francisco.

10 Law and disorder

The high excitement of sailing through the Golden Gate, after long, weary, monotonous weeks at sea, was shattered almost as soon as the newcomer set foot ashore. He found a city of flimsy tents and shacks, streets ankle deep in dust or impassable—"not even jackassable"—with mud. The residents looked dirty and unkempt. Prices were fantastically high, shortages frequent. Wrote one gold seeker after landing: "Just arrived—San Francisco be damned! Further particulars in my next."

When Vicente Perez Rosales reached San Francisco in February, 1849, he found no sidewalks, the center of the street "a slough of trampled mud." Piles of brush and tree limbs, bottles, discarded bales of tobacco, spoiled provisions, and every kind of debris were dumped into the muddy streets in an effort to provide solid footing. Holes that couldn't be filled were bridged with planks. Along the streets goods of all kinds were displayed in open array or under a flimsy tent. All around, the sound of sawing and hammering and building provided a background to the Babel of tongues that hammered on the ear.

With the help of great, sweeping fires, the city was built and rebuilt several times over. Tents and shacks gave way to wooden and adobe buildings, then to brick and cement. Streets were graded and planked, sewers started. At first, the new population clung to the curve of the beach, then gradually climbed the sandy hills and stretched beyond Rincon and Clark's Point. To the south, along the line of Market Street, tent cities grew up on the sand hills in Happy Valley and, not far away, Pleasant Valley. A plank road soon linked California Street with Mission Street and the Mission Dolores area.

The city pushed out, too, into the waters of the bay. Clark extended his wharf at the foot of Broadway 547 feet into the water. In 1849, Central or Long Wharf jutted 800 feet from the end of Commercial Street. Other wharves stretched into the bay at almost every street from California to Broadway. Buildings were erected on wharves, then on piles in between. The cove soon disappeared under the new piers. Ships abandoned in the bay were moved into permanent anchorages, converted into stores, warehouses, hotels. Many simply sank to the bottom and were covered with sand hauled down from the surrounding hills. The brig *Euphemia* was converted into the city's first jail. The *Niantic's* oak hull could be entered from Clay Street, under the sign, "Rest for the Weary & Storage for Trunks." Twenty years later, a rock and concrete seawall along the water front stabilized the city's shore line. Today, much of the city's financial district and many of its great buildings stand on ground reclaimed from the bay.

A quarter of a million dollars of gold reached San Francisco in an eight-week period in 1848. By the end of the year, the total came to close to 3 million. Then production skyrocketed: 25 million dollars in 1849, 60 million in 1850, 65 million in 1853. At first merchants and hotelkeepers treated gold dust rather gingerly, offering only $6 to $8 an ounce. Gamblers refused to play for the dust, insisting on hard money. The price, though, finally settled at $16 an ounce and coin of any other kind quickly grew scarce. Gold for years was the city's money.

The insatiable demand for supplies in the diggings, coupled with the rapid expansion of population, created a vast market where none had been before. Men made fortunes serving the mounting needs of the miners and the new population. Stores sprang up and freighters were soon hauling goods into the mining camps. Demand pushed back down the line, back to sources of food and materials and manufactured articles wherever in the world they might be found. "The riches of the Californian mines on the one side," an observer noted, "and the luxuries and conveniences of all countries in the world on the other, met in San Francisco."

Sheep were driven in from New Mexico and Chihuahua. Lumber was hauled from Puget Sound and, later, the California coast. From Oregon came eggs and vegetables and grain. Dried beef was sailed in from Chile. Cattle herds were driven in from Texas, and soon the state's own lands were trampled by the hooves of expanding herds. The demand for flour and grain put thousands of acres under cultivation. From the east coast and from Europe, around the Horn, came tons of manufactured supplies.

Industry, too, followed the trail. Wagonmaking and hide-tanning sprang up. Textile mills turned out woolens and grain sacks. Ironworking plants poured out a stream of equipment and machinery. Cabins, sluices, piling, and building of every kind created a hungry appetite for lumber.

Gold and the new industries soon gathered in San Francisco a bewildering conglomerate of people. The school commission in March, 1848, counted a total of 812 people. By the end of 1849 the population reached close to 25,000. By 1860, it was 57,000, the nation's fifteenth largest city. The Chinese were the largest national group among its motley people; the Irish, English, and Germans only slightly less numerous. Half of the population were foreign-born and considerably more had at least one foreign-born parent. A contemporary historian thought them "the wildest, bravest, most intelligent, yet most reckless and perhaps dangerous beings ever before collected into one small district of country."

The city pulsed with energy. Breakfast bells sounded almost with the first light of day. Moments later, it seemed, the air was filled with the racket of men at work. With morning mist still graying the skies, the streets began to fill with people. They "bustled and jostled against each other, bawled, railed, and fought, cursed, and swore, sweated and labored lustily," a historian observed, "and somehow the work was done." They bought and sold town lots and beach and water lots, shiploads of every kind of merchandise, gold dust in hundred weights, and great ranches, square leagues in extent, with thousands of cattle. They speculated in beef or flour, dry goods and wet, hard goods and soft.

People seemed always on the move. Unless they were deskbound, the streets were their marketplace, salesroom, clubroom, with an endless tide of people flooding through them. They had no homes as such—only boardinghouses or hotels. Some were miserable hovels, a few of a "superior class." They ate mainly in restaurants, in a dozen languages —French, Italian, Southern, Spanish, Chinese. Kitchen gardens soon put an abundance of fresh vegetables on dinner tables. The streams and hills and valleys beyond added salmon, cartloads of geese and ducks, all manner of wild fowl, bear, elk, deer, as well as smaller game and an abundance of beef.

Social center of the bustling town was the saloon and gambling hall. Any time of night or day, these were the likely spots to pick up the latest news, the spiciest gossip, to make a business deal or merely pass the night hours. Down the years they grew bigger, brighter, more elaborate. The town's social life was filled out, almost from the start, with theaters, occasional concerts and lectures. Balls and masquerades made the nights even gayer. Picnics on the sand hills back of town or across the bay, visits to the presidio or the mission, filled Sundays.

Most men carried a gun or a bowie knife. Violent quarrels were common, and duels, a historian wrote, "fearfully great." Personal disputes were frequently settled with revolvers, often with as much damage to spectators as to participants. "With shame it must be confessed," a historian noted, the general population of San Francisco drank heavily of intoxicating liquors and took its excitement "bold and reckless."

It was for a time almost a womanless society. The ratio of women to men at one point was one—or less—to a thousand. One woman wrote back home of the need for women.

"Some of the most ugly and slovenly servants here marry traders who have accumulated fortunes in a few weeks. A woman who comes here with one tooth in her head, has a great capital on the matrimonial line."

1852, said *The Annals of San Francisco,* a contemporary history, was the same "old dizzy round." Only now, there were more people, greater wealth, finer houses, more shops and stores, more work, more trade and profits. There were more saloons and more drunkenness, but there were also more benevolent institutions and orphans' asylums, more fire companies, more fraternal organizations, more newspapers and more churches—"more of everything that was beautiful and bad." By 1853, another observer reported, old settlers were looking back on the boisterous city of "old"— that remote period of four or five years back. Forty-niners were organizing a society of pioneers, staid citizens were patronizing Chinese laundries and putting their money in a bank.

But government left much to be desired. John W. Geary, postmaster and *alcalde,* let his fellow citizens in 1849 know just where they stood: "We are without a dollar in the public treasury and it is to be feared that the city is greatly in debt. You have neither an office for your magistrate nor any other public edifice. You are without a single police officer or watchman, and have not the means of confining a prisoner for an hour; neither have you a place to shelter, while living, sick and unfortunate strangers who may be cast upon our shores, or to bury them when dead. . . . In short, you are without a single requisite necessary for the promotion of prosperity, for the protection of property, or for the maintenance of order."

Efforts of local citizens to establish their own government were sharply rebuffed but General Bennett Riley, the military governor, quickly called a state constitutional convention. Under the new constitution, the legislature in the spring of 1850 granted a charter to the city of San Francisco. It vested power in a mayor and city council; the *alcalde* and *ayuntamiento* "passed out forever."

In late October, 1850, the steamer *Oregon* sailed through the Gate, her guns firing repeated prearranged signals. So it was that San Franciscans learned that, two months before, California had been admitted to the Union. Even before the ship rounded Clark's Point, the city began celebrating. Guns were fired, bonfires lighted on the hills, rockets blasted into the air. A parade, gaudy with banners and flags, accompanied by booming guns and fireworks, marked the day. The parading and speeches and noisy celebrating was topped that evening by "the grandest public ball that had yet been witnessed." Five hundred gentlemen and three hundred ladies "danced and made merry, till daylight."

Civil government came none too soon. In 1849, the city had been the victim of a gang of rowdies calling themselves the "Hounds" or "Regulators." No effective police power existed to resist them. Under a semblance of military discipline they raided saloons and stores, stole or destroyed anything valuable. A particularly cruel and violent raid on the inoffensive residents of "little Chile" finally ended the citizens' patience. With Sam Brannan in the forefront, they formed a grand jury and charged nineteen members of the gang with crimes against the people. Nine were found guilty and, though the jury talked of hanging, they were finally shipped out of the country.

Six great fires swept the town in the next eighteen months. The first on Christmas Eve, 1849, wiped out property worth many hundreds of thousands of dollars. Even greater conflagrations—three in 1850, two more in 1851—burned down block after block of buildings. Damage mounted close to 20 million dollars. Still, new buildings were started, as one observer noted, while the old sites "were hot with smoking ashes."

Some citizens came to believe, though, that at least part of the fires were set as a cover for robbery and plunder. The fifth great fire in May, 1851, set the merchants and mechanics talking. They set up informal patrols but these were inadequate. In June, the call went out to form a Committee of Vigilance. Sam Brannan figured large in the Committee. A close observer was a prominent merchant named William T. Coleman. In short order, some two hundred citizens were enrolled. Within hours, they brought in an unfortunate robber named Jenkins. He had been nabbed while attempting to row away from a store on the Long Wharf with a safe that did not belong to him. The Committee promptly tried him and found him guilty. That night he was hanged from a beam of the old custom house veranda.

In three months, the Vigilantes seized ninety-one men suspected of lawbreaking. They hanged four, banished twenty-eight. Some hundreds of others, they claimed, fled or went into hiding. Their work, they said, was to strengthen civil authorities, not to supersede them. They were interested only in the general good of the community. "Comparative peace," said a contemporary observer, "was restored."

But the peace did not last. Corruption infected city government. In 1856, public officials were charged with laxity in enforcing the laws, scandals in public works, manipulating elections. James King of William, editor of the recently launched *Bulletin,* published bold charges of corruption. He named men, specified their misdeeds, and called for action. One target was Supervisor James P. Casey. King claimed Casey was a former inmate of Sing Sing who had stuffed the ballot box to win election. Casey claimed King refused to print evidence disproving the charge. He provoked a street fight and shot King down.

Next day the Committee of Vigilance was revived, headed this time by William T. Coleman, who had taken part in the 1851 Committee. The Vigilantes enrolled some nine thousand members, set up a headquarters in a fortified warehouse called Fort Gunnybags—a tribute to the earth-filled bags that formed a breastworks around the place. The Vigilantes marched on the city jail, planted a cannon at the door, and gave the jailer ten minutes to give up Casey and a second prisoner, Charles E. Cora. The authorities turned over the two men, who were promptly tried and convicted. As a bell began tolling for the funeral procession of the dead editor, the Vigilantes hanged Casey and Cora.

Local officials, many lawyers and judges, along with state officials and other prominent citizens, joined a Law and Order Committee in opposition to the Vigilantes. General William Tecumseh Sherman was appointed to head the Law and Order military forces, but the Army's Department of California refused to provide arms or men. Sherman denounced the Vigilantes, in the words of Supreme Court Justice David Terry, as "a set of damned pork-merchants."

The Vigilantes, meanwhile, worked their way down a long list of suspected wrongdoers. They banished some, turned over others to the regular courts where they were promptly convicted. The neat efficiency of the operation inspired similar, though often less scrupulous, committees in cities and towns throughout the state.

When the Vigilantes completed what they conceived to be their work, they staged a mammoth parade of some six thousand armed men, threw open Fort Gunnybags to a public reception, then adjourned. But not, as it turned out, permanently.

11   And later . . .

San Francisco real estate, in that weird summer of 1848, had been worthless. But the demands of a mushrooming population quickly pushed land values to towering heights. A lot that sold for $12 plus filing fees on Vioget's map brought a few hundred dollars in late 1848, $6,000 in the spring of 1849, $45,000 in the fall. A little house of four rooms rented for $400 a month. Merchants paid $1,000 to $6,000 for stores. Gamblers gladly paid $10,000 a month rent for the lower floor of the Parker House.

Other prices soared no less astronomically. Walter Colton, onetime *alcalde* of Monterey and a major figure in writing the state's constitution, remembered his return from the mines in 1848. "You are hungry—want a breakfast—turn into a restaurant—call for ham and eggs and coffee—then your bill—six dollars! Your high boots, which have never seen a brush since you first put them on, have given out; you find a new pair . . . the price—fifty dollars!" A man paid $4, he said, for a haircut with dull shears and a shave with a razor stropped on the barber's boot. Good board cost $30 a week or $8 a day, a good meal $2 to $5. It was often cheaper to throw away clothes rather than pay $12 to $20 to have them laundered. A man paid $1 for a pill, the same for an egg. A brick cost a dime, common tacks sold for $5 to $10 an ounce. One ingenious newcomer put toothpicks on sale at 25 cents a dozen. When he saw how fast they were selling, he upped the price to 50 cents and quickly sold out his meager supply.

Labor, too, commanded a premium. "The daily laborer," reported the *Annals,* "who had worked for the good and at the command of another, for one or two dollars a day, could not be restrained from flying to the happy spot where he could earn six or ten times the amount . . . and the miner was his own master. . . . No man would give another a hand's turn for less than five dollars; while a day's constant labor of the commonest kind, if it could have been procured at all, would cost from twenty to thirty dollars, at least." Wages soared to levels that were not reached again in half a century and more.

Many, of course, found no gold. They went back to work at their old trades. Faced now with fantastically high prices, they demanded higher pay. Often they walked out on strike. They organized unions to obtain wages they considered fair. House carpenters in San Francisco and Sacramento struck in 1849 for $16 a day—California's first recorded strike. They went back to work for $13 with the promise of another dollar a day later. (Among the thirty "carpenters" who struck were three preachers, three physicians, six book-keepers, two lawyers.) Sailors, musicians, teamsters, and printers were a few of the trades involved in labor disputes.

The city's rapid expansion created countless jobs, but pay levels began to fall. Bricklayers, stonecutters, ship carpenters, made $10 a day in 1853; house carpenters and blacksmiths, $9. Shoemakers were paid $100 a month with board, teamsters $100 to $120. A common laborer earned $3.50 to $5 a day. Though these wages were well below those of '49, they were still several times higher than in the Atlantic states. Thousands of workers, often hungry and broke, willing to work at any wage, continued to pour into the city. With more men than jobs, wages fell steadily.

The city's boisterous prosperity slowed down even more in the winter of 1853–54. Gold production reached a peak and started to decline. The flood of immigrants thinned. Hundreds of miners, finding the diggings unprofitable, returned to the city. Merchants, unable to sell their stock or pay for merchandise they had ordered months before, closed their doors. Hundreds went broke. Real estate values crashed, loans went unpaid, banks collapsed. In a sense the Gold Rush ended here. The excitement, the feverish activity, and the fabulous profits dribbled out. San Francisco would again ride great waves of exciting, get-rich-quick prosperity, but never quite as high, quite as exciting, or quite as rich as in these early years.

The city came to know, too, destitution, sickness, and death from want and exposure. Immigrants landed who were sickly, emaciated, ill from scurvy or other diseases. Disappointed and empty-handed diggers swelled the city's destitute. They lived where they could, sleeping often on bare earth. Jobs, plentiful at first, became more difficult to find as business slowed down. Public meetings raised money for relief; churches and fraternal organizations formed societies to help out.

Now, too, the crude, roughshod democracy of the diggings faded. It had probably never been as widespread nor as democratic as had been claimed. Now it became even narrower. Workers returned to work, no longer their own masters, "for the good and at the command of another." They found they were forced to fight for a place in this rapidly shifting, mushrooming society. They had to fend off, somehow, the inevitable pressures pushing down on their wages. Increasingly, too, the opportunity to participate was narrowed. The Indian, the Mexican, the Chileno (the catalog label for most South Americans), along with the Chinese and black Americans, faced growing restrictions and rising barriers.

White miners had felt threatened by the Chinese work gangs they saw around them. The coolies worked for a few dollars and a bowl of rice. Even worse, they worked—not for themselves—but for others. Slave labor, too, at first represented an unfair and unequal advantage in the competition for gold and, later, for jobs. Competing with the poverty-stricken coolie or the enslaved black, the miner felt, could only drag him down to their mean levels. He reacted both illegally and legally, peacefully and violently.

Chinese in the gold fields were beaten, robbed, cheated, murdered. Threats of violence drove them from some camps; in others they could work only abandoned or unwanted claims. The saying, "not a Chinaman's chance," measured the Chinese miners' opportunity in the typical gold camp.

Black Americans, too, met similar treatment. Some were free men. Others were slaves brought by Southern owners to dig gold—although the owners were quickly stopped from working their claims with slaves. A few were runaways, seeking escape from fugitive slave laws. Blacks were often barred from owning or even working claims. Some stuck it out and a few struck it rich. But most, like the Chinese and other nonwhites, left the diggings to work in Sacramento or San Francisco. In the early fifties, many more stayed in the city than went to the mines—deterred by reports of white antagonism, color barriers, lack of opportunity.

The Chinese, with the free blacks, the *Annals* reported, performed any menial work "American males would scorn to do for any consideration." The *Annals* added, "The 'greasers,' too, who are verily 'of the earth, earthy,' helped the 'celestials' and the black fellows, or 'infernals' in their dirty work."

The state's new constitution prohibited slavery. It also denied the right to vote to "Indians, Africans and descendants of Africans," and, by extension, other nonwhites. The law allowed an Indian to be declared a vagrant on the say-so of any citizen and his services sold as a laborer for as much as four months. The "vagrant" received only his keep. Similarly, an Indian child, with his parents' consent, could be bound over to an employer for a specified period, much as an apprentice might be indentured to a master. The Indian child was seldom taught a trade, though, and was provided with no more than a miserable subsistence. Not infrequently, these arrangements resulted in kidnaping and virtual peonage.

The 1850 Legislature imposed a $20 a month tax on noncitizens for the right to dig for gold. It was enforced only occasionally against Frenchmen, Spanish-Americans, Indians, blacks, but frequently against Chinese. The tax was later reduced, but it was twenty years before it was held unconstitutional. A tax on fishing rights was similarly enforced. In 1855, the Legislature imposed a head tax of $50 on Chinese immigrants. In 1858, it prohibited their entry into the state. Both laws were later ruled unconstitutional, but they were the forerunners of half a century of efforts to restrict Chinese participation in San Francisco's society.

Courts in pre-Civil War California could not make up their minds what to do about runaway slaves. A number were freed, but some were returned to their owners. In 1852, the Legislature adopted a law requiring runaway slaves to be restored to their masters. In 1857, the State Supreme Court ruled that the slave Archy Lee was in fact free, but, since this was the first opportunity the court had had to pass on the question, he must be returned to his master. Many were angered by the ruling; it gave the law to the North, they said, but the slave to the South. Mary Pleasant, a prominent black woman who had contributed sizable sums of money to John Brown's foray at Harper's Ferry, led the city's black citizens in raising the money to buy Lee his freedom. The decision, nevertheless, ended legal sanction of slavery.

The 1850 Legislature also considered, though it did not adopt, a bill barring immigration of blacks. It did restrict service in the state militia to "whites only." But the Legislature provoked a deep anger when it barred the testimony of Indians and blacks (and later, Chinese) in any court action involving white persons.

San Francisco's tiny black population organized the Franchise League in 1852 in an effort to end the denial of their right to vote. (Their efforts echoed the fight then raging in the eastern states to end slavery.) Mifflin Wistar Gibbs, later the nation's first black municipal judge, Jonas

P. Townsend, and W. H. Newby were among those spurring the protest. They joined, too, soon after in publishing *Mirror of the Times,* the city's first black publication.

In 1855, forty-nine blacks from ten counties met in Sacramento in the first "Convention of the Colored Citizens of the State of California." Their principal anger was directed at the denial of their right to testify in court, though it also expressed concern with problems of education and legal equality. The Convention met again in 1857 and 1862, but its efforts to modify or repeal the ban on testimony gained little ground. They were frustrated by the fact that the law had been aimed far more at the numerous Chinese and Indians than at the blacks. Without it, a court ruling in 1856 held, "the European white man . . . would not be shielded from the testimony of the degraded and demoralized caste [the Chinese], while the Negro, fresh from the coast of Africa, the Indian of Pantagonia, the Kanaka [native of Hawaii], South Sea Islander, or New Hollander, would be admitted . . . to testify against white citizens." If the law were repealed, the ruling said, it would admit them to equal rights of citizenship and they would soon appear in the jury box, on the bench, and in the Legislature.

Opponents of the law complained that it made them defenseless targets of violence and robbery, unable to testify in their own defense or in defense of others who were attacked or injured. "Any white man can swear a Chinaman's life away in the courts," Mark Twain summed up, "but no Chinaman can testify against a white man."

In 1852, the Legislature refused, 47 to 1, even to receive a petition from the Franchise League. A second petition was greeted with a motion to throw it out of the window. The motion was ruled out of order but the clerk was instructed not to file the petition. In 1863, with the political power of the Southerners blotted out by the Civil War, the Legislature amended the law to allow blacks to testify. Passage of the 15th Amendment after the Civil War opened the way for blacks to vote. The final racial bars to testimony in court were dropped in 1873.

Segregated schools for black children were the rule almost from the start. When James B. Sanderson, a black himself, reached San Francisco in 1853, he found no black youth in the schools. Under his leadership, the first school for black youngsters was opened in 1854 in the basement of a church. Sanderson was instrumental, too, in establishing separate schools in Sacramento and Stockton. Segregation was probably not total, however.

A political contest in 1858 produced a campaign charge that "Negroes were taught and classed upon terms of equality." The school superintendent admitted that in fact blacks were "classed upon terms of equality with white children" in three schools. The Board of Education promptly ruled that "no colored children would be admitted to any public school except a school for colored children." Black citizens, though, continued to campaign against segregation. They won their first success when the Legislature in 1874 decided that "colored children could attend a white school if no colored school existed." Black parents balked at the dual system and succeeded in 1875 in eliminating it from the law. Segregation in fact continued for generations, though, despite the law.

In 1859, twenty-four years after his first visit, Richard Henry Dana came back to San Francisco. "We bore round the point toward the old anchoring-ground of the hide ships," he wrote, "and there, covering the sand hills and the valleys, stretching from the water's edge to the base of the great hills, and from the old Presidio to the Mission, flickering all over with the lamps of its streets and houses, lay a city of one hundred thousand inhabitants." (It was, in fact, only fifty-seven thousand.) As Dana explored the city, comparing it with his recollections of Yerba Buena in 1835, measuring the vast changes, "I could scarcely keep my hold on reality."

The changes were vast. People of all kinds lived together, though, too often, merely side by side. Common hardship, common shortages, common wants, forged a pattern of closeness, born in the gold fields and tolerated in the city by an easygoing, hard-working, often hard-drinking society. Another tradition, also with roots in the gold fields, made outcasts of the nonwhite, abused and tortured the Chinese, the Indian, the Mexican, the black. These varied strands were woven together in bright, often harsh and conflicting patterns, in which the separate tones became lost—visible only by looking hard and close.

12   The silver-plated city

San Francisco celebrated completion of the transcontinental railroad on May 8, 1869—two days before it was completed. Told that the ceremony of driving the last spike would be delayed to Monday, local officials refused to put off their festivities; Saturday, they said, was a better day for celebrating. So they did: a thundering salute at sunrise, flags and banners whipping in the breeze, a massive four-hour parade. Even while the paraders were still marching, Judge Nathaniel Bennett, orator of the day, according to the *Bulletin,* spellbound his listeners at Mechanics' Pavilion for two hours. Two days later, Governor Leland Stanford, using a silver-plated sledge hammer, drove the final, golden spike into a tie of California laurel. "The last rail is laid, the last spike is driven. The Pacific railroad is finished," the officials telegraphed President U. S. Grant.

The prospects left the *Bulletin* openmouthed. Soon, it wrote, one would be able to travel from ocean to ocean in six days, to London or Paris, perhaps, in fifteen to seventeen days. San Francisco anticipated a renewed influx of immigrants, along with a fresh and boundless prosperity. On the other hand, Henry George, a San Francisco newspaperman who would one day be a candidate for mayor of New York (and win more votes than Theodore Roosevelt), predicted it would quickly build a "populous empire," but it would also bring wealth to a few, destitution to many.

In fact, completion of the railroad ushered in a period of depression and unemployment, of conflict and friction, wild financial speculation, the rise of great and powerful monopolies, a violent crusade against the Chinese.

It also closed an era. From the beginning, San Francisco had been cut off—isolated from the rest of the world by long weeks and months of hard and clumsy travel. Much of what she was reflected her isolation. Now it had ended. San Francisco had finally joined the Union.

For a quarter of a century before, while men talked of bridging the continent with a railroad, communication was awkwardly maintained with clipper ship and stage line, pony express and telegraph. Theodore D. Judah, brilliant young engineer who had built the state's first railroad, developed detailed plans for laying rails across the towering Sierra and for forming the Central Pacific Railroad. Rebuffed in San Francisco, he enlisted a number of Sacramento storekeepers: Collis Huntington, Leland Stanford, Mark Hopkins, Charles Crocker, who, in time, were dubbed the Big Four. With Judah's lobbying, urged on by the Civil War, Congress authorized the Pacific railroad. The Central Pacific group would build eastward from Sacramento; the Union Pacific would lay the eastern link westward from the Missouri River. Each completed mile of track became a valuable prize, rewarding the builder with a four-foot right-of-way along with 12,800 acres of public lands. Government money helped to finance the job.

Charles Crocker, construction boss for the Big Four, laid the first rail in 1863. Almost from the start he was plagued by man-power troubles. Few men were willing for very long to tackle the rugged work for $1 a day and board. Crocker was appalled when it was suggested he hire Chinese to build his railroad. He had rarely seen one over five feet tall or weighing more than 120 pounds. His partners doubted that the small, wiry Chinese could endure rugged construction work. In 1865 Crocker gave in and hired his first Chinese crew. His white employees complained that the Chinese crew's low pay would drag their own down. Crocker insisted the Chinese were the answer: white workers who could not get along with them could quit.

Crocker's first Chinese workers dispelled any doubts. They learned quickly, worked methodically and energetically. He tried them on grading. They turned in the longest, smoothest stretch of any crew on the line. Crocker hired more Chinese. He recruited them throughout the state, then contracted with shipping firms to hire and transport them directly from China. By 1869, he had close to fifteen thousand Chinese building his railroad. In the final climactic days of the heated competition with the Union Pacific, crews of Chinese workers laid more than ten miles of track in a twelve-hour shift—a world record outstripping any achieved by boastful Union Pacific crews. When the road was completed, Crocker paid tribute to "that poor, destitute class of laborers called Chinese." Their "fidelity and industry," he said, were in great measure responsible for early completion of the railroad.

Meantime, San Francisco was sailing high on the crest of

another boom. In 1859, near a mining camp called John-town, on the Nevada (the eastern) slope of the Sierra, Pete O'Riley and Pat McLaughlin had turned up a strange blue substance in the sand they were washing for gold. One night, old Pancake Comstock saw the stuff. It was silver ore, he told Pete and Pat; they had struck it rich. They formed the Ophir Company and staked out the first claim on what came to be called the Comstock Lode. Soon, miners, prospectors, would-be fortune hunters, were clambering over the Sierras into Nevada, this time looking for the strange blue stuff.

But silver mining was no one-man job; it called for heavy equipment and capital. To raise the money they needed, miners sold shares in their prospective bonanzas. The way was thus opened for some of the wildest stock market spec-ulation the country had ever seen. Some stocks were worth-less; the market was frequently rigged, but San Franciscans bought and sold silver shares wildly. Every report of a rich strike or of increased production sent prices soaring.

Samuel L. Clemens, only then becoming known as Mark Twain, recalled how practically everyone—"bankers, mer-chants, lawyers, doctors, mechanics, laborers, even the very washerwoman and servant-girl"—put every penny he or she could raise into silver stocks. "What a gambling carnival it was!" Twain himself looked forward to the day he would be-come a millionaire simply by cashing his stock. Then the bottom fell out; countless "millionaires" were ruined. Twain mourned, "I was an early beggar and a thorough one. My hoarded stocks were not worth the paper they were printed on. I threw them all away."

Silver production in 1860 amounted to $116,000; it soared to $1,547,000 in the next year, and kept climbing.

The help of California's gold and silver to the Union cause in the Civil War quickly assumed great importance. Union supporters worried that the stream of riches might be turned to the South. One group of Southern sympathizers loaded a schooner with arms and ammunition, had her towed into the bay ready to sail. But somehow their plans for seizing government installations and arms and raiding Union ships leaked out. As the sun rose next morning, the schooner found herself under the guns of a U.S. gunboat, with boatloads of marines rowing toward her.

By 1870, silver production reached 17 million dollars and was still growing. Some people thought the Comstock was worked out; others were buying up mines with all their resources. Countless mine operators borrowed heavily from William C. Ralston and William Sharon and their Bank of California. Ralston and Sharon poured millions into mills and mines, convinced that new bonanzas would be found. In 1871, the Virginia & California mine struck a fabulously rich fifty-four foot vein, worth, it was claimed, anywhere from 117 to 300 million dollars.

Once more, stock speculation skyrocketed. A vague rumor that the Virginia & California had exhausted its vein sent stock prices crashing, losing over 24 million dollars almost overnight. The market recovered but plummeted again in 1875 when word got around that the Bank of California was in trouble, scratching for funds to meet its obligations. It collapsed with a resounding crash.

Sharon, Darius Ogden Mills, and others managed to scramble clear of the crash and rescue their fortunes. Ralston was not so fortunate. This energetic pioneer had buillt the fabled Palace Hotel, developed a great estate down the peninsula at Belmont, helped to organize the Spring Valley Water Company. Few San Francisco enterprises of the time did not know the Ralston touch. When the bank crashed, he nevertheless went to North Beach for his customary afternoon swim. By accident—or design?—he drowned.

On the ruins of his bank, though, other Nevada millionaires erected a new bank and tightened their hold on the Comstock. In time the lode was exhausted and Virginia City, once its capital, became a ghost town. But the fabulous Comstock produced fortunes for the Mackays, Fairs and Floods, the O'Briens, Sharons, Mills, the Jones, Sutro, Hearst families—and more. It provided nearly twenty years of excitement and hope and disappointment and had pumped millions into the economy of the region and of the nation.

The flood of wealth—from the gold mines of the Sierra foothills, the Nevada silver mines, the flourishing Central Pacific, booming trade—poured into San Francisco. "A man may make his fortune in the desert of Nevada or Idaho," an old-timer said, "but he is pretty sure to spend it in San Francisco."

Jim Flood, a Montgomery street saloonkeeper who had invested heavily in silver, built a fabulous castle on Nob Hill, enclosing it in a $30,000 brass fence. Mark Hopkins, one of the Central Pacific's Big Four, built an imitation castle diagonally across the street from the Flood mansion. Terraced gardens fell away on the steep hillside at back, surrounded by a forty-foot wall. Hopkins' partner, Leland Stanford, senator, governor, founder of a university, built just below the Hopkins castle. Ralston had his house nearby. Charles Crocker's $2,300,000 place covered most of the block. The writer Gertrude Atherton commented that it

looked as if several architects had worked on it and "fought
one another to a finish."

It was an Arabian Nights era, wrote Julia Cooley Altroc-
chi, of "sultanic palaces, fantastic towers, gold dinner services, silver balustrades and doorknobs, Oriental carpets, Chinese brocades, marquetry, parquetry, Pompeian frescoes,
South African diamonds, rainbow apparel, extravagance and
extravaganza."

San Francisco was a town, a visitor noted, of "bummers."
"Nowhere else can a worthless fellow, too lazy to work, too
cowardly to steal, get on so well." He could sleep outdoors
and live off the free lunch. Chief among the "bummers"
probably was Emperor Norton I, who had lost his fortune
and his sanity in a vain attempt to corner the rice market.
The Emperor issued frequent pronouncements and procla-
mations (including one ordering construction of a bridge
across the bay). He issued his own currency which, in reasonably small quantities, was accepted by merchants and
saloonkeepers. He was sometimes accompanied by Bummer
and Lazarus, a pair of disreputable dogs who had set aside
selected kitchens and saloons along Montgomery Street as
their private preserve.

Mark Twain wrote of these years in Virginia City, the
Mother Lode Country, and San Francisco. His was a laugh-
ing, teasing, often biting picture. Bret Harte, editor of the
Californian and later of the *Overland Monthly,* wrote tales
of gold camps and gold miners that painted the pioneer's red
shirt romantic and his muddy boots heroic. The two—Harte
and Twain—were the forerunners of a strong, vital, and
characteristic San Francisco literary tradition.

A historian wrote of this period: "Nowhere else will such

bad manners be found in families possessing so much wealth." Their fortunes, he noted, came "by bold investments or lucky speculations, and not by occupations requiring much erudition or refinement."

Harte sneered at the displays of wealth. "Shoddy is here," he said, "and California shoddy at that."

13   Another "Jonah"

It seemed for a while in the sixties as if there were almost enough wealth to go around. Gold and silver poured in an endless flood from mines on both sides of the Sierra, creating in turn an enormous appetite for machinery and supplies. The Central Pacific was making its rocky way over the mountains and out on to the Nevada desert. Capital was plentiful and usually quickly and profitably invested. Labor was scarce and jobs were plentiful. Workers in more than a score of crafts organized into unions and demanded higher pay and an eight-hour day. Striking for higher pay, the *Bulletin* commented, "is now the rage among the working people. . . . But great care should be taken not to overdo the thing."

Completion of the transcontinental railroad in 1869 turned loose thousands of construction workers, many of them Chinese. Immigrants poured in from the East, often penniless and anxious to work. Eastern merchants dumped tons of merchandise on the local market. Stores were soon overstocked. The city's new subdivisions went unsold. Land values fell, prices collapsed, exports decreased, factories closed. Several thousand workers were idle in San Francisco; from 50,000 to 100,000 were reported without work in the state. With a vast oversupply of workers, ready and willing to work, employers cut wages and wiped out the eight-hour day.

"Where there is discontent, if there is not one Jonah, another will be found," observed Henry George. ". . . the presence of the Chinese has largely engrossed the attention of the laboring classes, offering what has seemed to them a sufficient explanation of the fall of wages and difficulty of finding employment."

There had been fewer than a thousand Chinese in California before 1850. Then they came in a great human torrent. Many left China by choice, some were virtually kidnaped. Most arrived heavily in debt for the cost of their voyage and bound to their sponsor. However they came, overwhelmingly they clung to the dream that one day they would return to their native village.

At first, they were a curiosity, strange and colorful. As their numbers grew, Americans found their habits and manners "repugnant," the *Annals* reported. "John" was considered inferior in "most mental and bodily qualities, nor does he smell very sweet"; the *Annals* added, "his lying knavery and natural cowardice are proverbial. . . . He is poor and mean, somewhat slavish and crouching. . . . They are nicknamed, cuffed about and treated very unceremoniously."

Mark Twain wrote a story for his newspaper of some Irish hoodlums stoning a Chinese laundryman, but his editor refused to print it. The paper, the editor explained, gathered "its livelihood from the poor and we must respect their prejudices or perish. The Irish were the poor . . . and they hated the Chinese."

Driven from the mines, the Chinese found jobs in the city in laundries, in garment factories, as household servants. They worked as fishermen, freight haulers, wood choppers. They were soon a sizable part of the work force in cigar factories and boot and shoe factories. Their employers, both Chinese and Occidental, exploited them without mercy. They were denounced as a threat to the jobs and living standards of white workers. They were condemned to live in cramped and crowded hovels, then excoriated for living there.

Repeated attempts were made to use the law to exclude Chinese from the San Francisco society. The miner's tax drove them from the mines. They were subjected for a time to an unconstitutional head tax. The shoulder pole they used to carry baskets and chairs was barred from the streets. They were threatened with a legal shearing of their treasured braids; no self-respecting Chinese would be seen without his queue dangling down his back. He was taxed if he used a horse to carry laundry, taxed if he did not. His testimony, like that of the Indian and black, was barred in court actions involving white persons. To wipe out crowded Chinese hovels, an ordinance was enacted requiring a minimum of 500 cubic feet of living space per adult. The number of arrests so overcrowded the city's jail that the city found itself violating its own ordinance.

Isolated by custom and religion, language and culture, exploited by employers of any color, the Chinese quickly became a target for anger and discontent in a labor market overrun by jobless men. But they were not the only target.

People were increasingly angered by the growing railroad monopoly; it held much of the state's best land, demanded heavy subsidies from towns along the main line, exploited the farmers who bought its land. People also resented the large-scale ranches that hired big gangs of men for a brief season, then dumped them, jobless, on the cities. Corruption in government, people said, meant that a short term in office could yield a lifetime of wealth. They resented unemployment, pay cuts, long hours.

When news reached San Francisco in the summer of 1877 of the great and violent railroad strikes sweeping the East, workingmen's groups called a sympathy meeting. They gathered on the sand lots at Larkin and Leavenworth and Market Streets, facing the City Hall then under "leisurely" construction. Thousands turned out in a quiet, orderly, good-natured protest—until someone cried out, "On to Chinatown!" The mob demolished a Chinese laundry with rocks and bricks. An overturned lamp set fire to a building and the crowd harassed the firemen working to bring it under control. Before the night was over, a score of Chinese laundries were wrecked, a liquor store looted, a church mission stoned, a plumbing shop demolished.

Next day, the third Committee of Safety was mobilized under William T. Coleman who had headed the Vigilantes of 1856. Committee members were armed with pickhandles, held to their wrists by leather thongs. That night they guarded a Mission Street woolen mill, but the crowd instead attacked some nearby Chinese laundries. On the third night, rumors hinted the mob would attempt to burn the Pacific

Mail docks where ships bearing Chinese immigrants cus-
tomarily landed. Instead, a lumberyard was set afire. Four
men were killed, fourteen wounded, and property exten-
sively damaged in the violence that ensued. After five days
order was restored and the pickhandle "Vigilantes" dismissed. The anger and discontent remained.

One of the men who carried a pickhandle was a drayman
named Dennis Kearney. Born in Ireland in 1847, he went to
sea at the age of eleven. He came to San Francisco in 1868
as first officer of a clipper ship. He worked for a time for a
steamship company, then bought into a drayage firm. For
two years he attended a Sunday-afternoon debating club in
search of self-improvement. He was noticed, Henry George
reported, only for the "bitter vulgarity of his attacks on religion" and "the venom with which he abused the working
classes."

When Kearney was refused membership in the Workingmen's Party of the United States, he organized his own. It
broke up, however, in a dispute over splitting the political
contributions it had collected. On September 16, 1877,
Kearney spoke at a sandlot meeting—first in a series that
raised this uneducated, ham-fisted drayman to great, if brief,
political power. In October, he formed—and became president of—the Workingmen's Party of California.

Kearney was a chunky man, with a broad head, a slight
mustache, blue eyes. He set off his thick, knotted fists and
jutting jaw with a drayman's copper-riveted, leather apron.
He denounced the "land monopoly" and "money power."
He charged Congress was manipulated by thieves, the Legislature ruled by land speculators and bribes. He recommended every workingman get himself a musket and a hun-

dred rounds of ammunition. "A little judicious hanging would be the best course to pursue with the capitalists," he suggested. "A few fires would clear the atmosphere." Deadliest of all was his repeated cry, "The Chinese must go!" a phrase he had borrowed from another speaker.

Kearney quickly became the target of the authorities. He and some of his followers were jailed—not once but several times. Both the Supervisors and the Legislature passed special laws in futile efforts to gag him. His party's statewide convention avoided police attack only by announcing one meeting place while the delegates gathered secretly at another. His party, one newspaper said, was "the uprising of an illiterate, alien mob of adventurers, agitators, and tramps, too lazy to work and too cowardly to steal, except as coyotes do, in packs in the night."

" 'John' must leave our shores—peaceably if possible, forcibly if necessary," Kearney told a sandlot crowd. His party proposed to rid the country of "John Chinaman"— the popular label of Chinese labor—and wrest government from the rich. Public lands would be held for settlement by individuals—not more than a square mile to a person. The eight-hour day would be established by law. Women would receive equal pay for equal work. The party would establish free, compulsory education and free textbooks for children under fourteen.

Kearney's party scored a series of quick, surprising election victories. It climaxed its successes by electing fifty delegates to the State Constitutional Convention of 1878. Its delegation was second only to the nonpartisan group, far larger than the Republicans and Democrats. The delegates, though, one reporter said, were "utterly ignorant" men, "de-

sirous of doing something for the laboring classes, without
the slightest idea of how to do it." They were frequently out-
maneuvered in convention proceedings both by business and
farm interests. They were fobbed off with a number of restrictions on the Chinese, most of them of highly doubtful
legality.

The new constitution was anything but a workingman's
document, Henry George observed; it was less than many
had hoped, but it was also more than some had wanted. The
people, in any case, ratified it. Soon after, Kearney's Workingmen's Party disintegrated and disappeared entirely within
a few years. Kearney himself tried a variety of jobs; in the
end an uncle left him a good deal of money. He died in Alameda in 1907.

Kearney and his party did win a hearing for the workingmen with the Democratic and Republican parties. They reflected, in an angry and incendiary way, both the problems
and power of working people. Perhaps their greatest legacy,
though, was to catapult the status of the Chinese into a national question. In 1878 Congress attempted to restrict Chinese immigration. President Hayes vetoed the measure as a
violation of the Burlingame Treaty with China, but he sent a
commission to negotiate a new understanding. In 1882, under a new treaty, Congress approved a temporary exclusion
which was made permanent soon after the turn of the century.

But the bitterness against the Chinese did not fade. They
found jobs on Central Valley farms, only to be driven off by
anti-Chinese riots in 1893 and 1894. They were excluded
from one industry after another. More and more they withdrew—under unrelenting pressure—into the impoverished

security of their own increasingly crowded quarter. Generations would be born and die before the Chinese, on the one hand, gave up their dream of returning home and the Americans, on the other, bridged the unreasoning bitterness and anger that stood between them.

14   The first major battle

"There is almost nothing to see in San Francisco worth seeing," commented Anthony Trollope, the famous English novelist, during a visit in 1875: a park, he noted, not yet completed; its biggest hotel—the Palace—completed but not yet opened. Strangers are taken to a place called the Cliff House to hear seals bark, he reported. Strangers will want to get away as quickly as they can.

"The youngest, freest, most talked-about city on earth," wrote a latter-day chronicler, ". . . famed for its beautiful women and high-tempered men, its French restaurants, free lunches, gourmands, gourmets, millionaires, political czars, Nob Hill and Barbary Coast. . . . The city that never slept."

San Francisco in the 1890's was a Sunday ride in the new Golden Gate Park on a bicycle built for two, a swank Hunt Ball at the Palace, summers in San Rafael or Del Monte or the mountains of San Mateo county, diamond-studded dog collars and thousand-dollar Paris gowns. San Francisco was a heart-tearing production of *Bertha, the Sewing Machine Girl* at Walter Morosco's Grand Opera House on Mission Street, where seats under the "largest chandelier in America" sold for as little as a dime.

San Francisco was the famed cocktail route—a score or more saloons along Kearny Street where each evening an impressive masculine parade made its bibulous way. Merchants and judges, politicians, bankers and newspaper men, socialites and lawyers, sampled the generous free lunch: Virginia ham baked in champagne, sweetbreads, alligator pears, venison, clams and shrimps, platters of cheese and sausages and salami. If a man was important enough, his drink was poured from his own bottle.

Wealthy San Franciscans drove prancing teams over the Cliff House road and their daughters competed for European titles. Lesser saloons on nearly every corner supplied recreation for the other San Francisco. Beer gardens, amusement parks, and picnic grounds catered to workingmen and their families and to the emerging middle class.

The literary tradition of Mark Twain and Bret Harte flourished. Ina Donna Coolbrith earned her living as a librarian—in Oakland, then later at the Mechanics-Mercantile and Bohemian Club libraries in San Francisco. She worked with Harte on the *Overland Monthly* and corresponded with Tennyson, Rossetti, Whittier, and other famous poets. In 1915 she was made the state's first poet laureate.

Helen Hunt Jackson was unimpressed with San Francisco; it was, she thought, hopelessly crowded and mixed and "can never look from the water like anything but a toppling town." Her books, the factual *A Century of Dishonor* and the romantic novel *Ramona,* focused angry, but short-lived, attention on American treatment of the Indian.

Ambrose Bierce waxed his fiercest. He had set out, he wrote, to instruct "such writers as it is worth while to instruct, and assassinate those that it is not." He carried out his mission with occasional rapier thrusts, more often with bludgeon-like blows. In 1913 he traveled to Mexico where he disappeared from sight and presumably died.

William Dozey's bookstore on Market Street near the Palace Hotel became the center of a young group of writers and artists calling themselves *Les Jeunes.* The group launched *The Lark* as a monthly outlet for their bursting literary ambitions. Gelett Burgess was a leading light among the group and *The Lark* is generously sprinkled with his verse and illustrations. He wrote:

> *I never saw a purple cow.*
> *I never hope to see one*
> *but I can tell you anyhow*
> *I'd rather see than be one.*

Later he regretted it:

> *Ah, yes, I wrote the "Purple Cow"—*
> *I'm sorry now I wrote it;*
> *But I can tell you anyhow*
> *I'll kill you if you quote it.*

The Lark was priced at 5 cents a copy, $1 a year—Burgess explained that he was never very good at arithmetic. It published the contributions of Bruce Porter, who went on to design stained-glass windows; Willis Polk who became an important designer; Maynard Dixon whose paintings remem-

bered the Old West; and more: Ernest Peixotto, Florence
Lundborg, Carolyn Wells. Just as *The Lark* seemed about
to succeed, the group killed it. "Our mood was too spon-
taneous or rather too enthusiastic . . . there was the
world's sober work to do," Burgess explained. He went on
to his own career as a novelist, humorist, comic cartoonist.

In the nineties, too, Hubert Howe Bancroft published the
last of the thirty-nine volumes of his *History of the Pacific
States.* Bancroft had set himself up in a "history factory."
A staff of assistants dug up and edited the raw materials
which Bancroft then fashioned into extensive and detailed
history. John L. Hittell, author of a four-volume history of
California, thought the Bancroft works unreliable—so much
so that he said he did not consult them in the course of his
own work. When Bancroft dubbed the Bear Flag episode
"a criminal revolt of vagabond settlers," the Society of California Pioneers indignantly drummed him out of its ranks.

In 1899 Frank Norris wrote *McTeague,* a work of unex-
pected and, for the time, surprising realism. Soon after came
the first two volumes of his planned trilogy on "The Epic
of Wheat." *The Octopus* recorded the fierce battle between
the railroad and the wheat farmers—a seldom-told chapter
in the state's history. Then came *The Pit.* Death cut short
Norris's plans.

Henry George, Philadelphia-born, worked as seaman,
steward, prospector, typesetter, day laborer, newspaper
reporter and journalist, economic theorist and crusader.
George watched land prices rise with the coming of the railroad and under the pressure of the growing population. He
combined his observations with his personal and intimate
acquaintance with poverty. From it he distilled the idea that

it was the community—the progress of civilization—that increased the value of land. The community, he concluded, ought to take back the wealth it created, instead of allowing it to fatten the purses of already wealthy landowners and spread poverty among the landless. He proposed a single tax on landowners to recapture the unearned increase in land values.

Publishers refused to touch his book, which he called *Progress and Poverty,* so George printed it himself, locally. He went on from San Francisco to a hectic career in the East, including two campaigns for the mayoralty of New York City. His book and his idea still hold the loyalty of thousands of followers around the world.

It was George, then editor of a San Francisco newspaper, who turned an early light on the abuse and exploitation of seamen that were part of the city's water-front life. He pointed an indignant editorial finger at the sailors' boardinghouse keepers who bore the unlovely title of "crimps." The arriving sailor found a warm welcome from the crimp. He was plied with liquor and women and clothing (all with a generous profit added)—anything the man wanted. The hospitality came to an abrupt halt, though, when the sailor's bill reached about as much as a man could earn on an ordinary voyage. Then he was sold—often for "blood money"— to the highest bidder among shipmasters preparing to sail. If the man-power pool ran low, men were often "shanghaied"—kidnaped and forcibly put aboard ship. The crimp was paid out of the seaman's earnings. From time to time, uptown businessmen and city officials poked into the crimping system, but it was usually indifferently done and quickly forgotten.

Seamen's wages and working conditions were left to the untender mercies of the crimps, of tough "bucko" mates and blustering ship captains. If a sailor quit his job, it was desertion. If he protested, it was mutiny. He lived at sea in dingy, airless, cramped "dogholes." He ate bad food, worked twelve to fourteen hours a day—and around the clock in bad weather. Several attempts to organize a union failed; when the members went to sea, there was nobody on shore to take care of the union's business. The answer to this dilemma, oddly enough, came from a landlubber.

Burnette G. Haskell was trained as a lawyer. For a short time he edited an erratic weekly newspaper called *Truth,* which served briefly as spokesman for the city's growing union movement. He organized his personal and local version of the International Workingmen's Association which Karl Marx had founded in Europe. With a handful of I.W.A. members he convened a dockside meeting one foggy March night in 1885, where the Coast Seamen's Union was organized. From this beginning stemmed the sturdy unionism of San Francisco's seafaring men. Haskell and his associates provided a shoreside committee to handle the union's problems while the members were at sea.

Soon a onetime clerk in an Oslo grocery store went to work for the union. His name was Andrew Furuseth, a sharp-nosed, ascetic, stubborn man who fought the sailors' fight for close to half a century. Always defiant, always proud, Furuseth told the shipowners and the government: "You can put me in jail. But you cannot give me narrower quarters than as a seaman I have always had. You cannot give me worse food than I have always eaten. You cannot make me lonelier than I have always been." Under his unyielding persistence, laws were gradually enacted that gave the seaman his economic freedom, that allowed him to organize, to strike, that protected his rights to fair wages and decent treatment. Under Furuseth, as under later leaders, the seamen fought many a battle to improve their lot and to protect their union. They lost some, won more. In the end they came back. "Tomorrow," Furuseth would say, "is another day."

As the seamen organized, so in the eighties did the men who worked in the uptown shops and mills and factories. The employers organized, too, into industry associations that confronted a lone union with the full breadth of the industry's owners. Wars promptly broke out. Hotel and restaurant owners broke the union of cooks and waiters. The shipowners tried to wrest control over hiring from the seamen's union. The iron founders demanded the men take a cut in pay and, when the men refused, imported strikebreakers from the East to fill their jobs. The employers forced a general lockout in the shoe industry; union workers were compelled to quit their union to get their jobs back.

The employers' association boasted in 1893 that it "can look with complacency upon its work during the last two years. One after another the unions have been taught a salutary lesson. . . ." A year later, the association bragged that "among the industries of San Francisco there remains but a single union which imposes its rules upon its trade."

The workers' plight was worsened by a bitter depression that swept the nation in 1893. Never, said the *Coast Seamen's Journal,* had San Francisco seen such destitution, misery, and suffering. Police stations provided hundreds with free meals and lodging. Soup kitchens, free employment bureaus, public woodyards, and street-sweeping gangs were organized to help the thousands of jobless men.

In the midst of the depression, though, San Francisco businessmen raised $350,000 to stage the lavish Columbian Exposition of 1894 in Golden Gate Park.

15 *The second battle*

The new century found San Francisco again on the up-swing. Hawaii had only recently been annexed to the United States, the Spanish-American War ended, the Philippines occupied. Gold had been found in the Yukon and the Klondike. New industries sprang up, old ones flourished; the vast markets of the Orient beckoned. San Francisco was the hustling, vigorous hub of this burgeoning world.

San Francisco's world, too, was changed, and changing. In the state's great central valley, the huge wheat and cattle ranches of the "bonanza" days were being broken up. Smaller farms were producing the increasingly specialized fruit and vegetable crops, as well as the livestock that would, in the years ahead, make it one of the world's richest valleys. Its produce poured through San Francisco's warehouses and over her docks. Much of it was processed and distributed by firms headquartered in San Francisco. Gold and silver had made the city financial headquarters of the West almost from the very start. Now her financial interests spread beyond mining into agriculture, transportation, manufacturing, finance.

The city's broadened economy was reflected in the jobs of her people. The 1900 census found nearly a third of her work force—some 56,000 people—working in trade and transportation. Nearly as many—52,000—worked in manufacturing. Domestic and personal service furnished jobs for 43,000; lawyers, doctors, and teachers made up the bulk of the city's 11,000 professional workers. At the time, 27,000 were jobless.

San Francisco had always drawn her population from many corners of the world. In 1900, the mix of nationalities and racial stocks was changing. The city's population totaled 342,782. Every third person was foreign-born. Three of every four had at least one foreign-born parent. The proportion of foreign-born would never be as high again. Germans were the most numerous among the city's 117,000 foreign-born. Ireland, England, the Scandinavian countries, and China contributed large numbers of the most recent arrivals. Some 17,000 were listed as "colored": 14,000 Chinese (over 10,000 of them born in China), 1,800 Japanese, 1,700 "persons of negro descent." The census identified only 15 American Indians. The Mexicans and the Spanish, with the assortment of racial backgrounds they had brought with them at the start, had disappeared into the mixture usually described as "native white."

Some colonies of the foreign-born, though represented from the times of the gold rush or before, were assuming increased importance. A small group of Jews had observed their High Holy Days in 1849 in a tent room on Jackson Street. Soon afterward, they had formed two congregations of their co-religionists: Temple Sherith Israel in 1850, Temple Emanu-El a year later. In 1850, the city's Jews formed the Eureka Benevolent Society "to assist those in need." In 1855 a bill in the State Legislature sought to impose a prohibitive tax on Jews. It was intended to halt them from observing their Sabbath on Saturday, then opening their stores for business on Sunday. The San Francisco *Chronicle* rushed to their defense, noting that they were not alone in doing business on the Christian Sabbath. The editorial argued that persecution or prejudice did not fit with the American boast of freedom. The census of 1900 did not identify the Jewish immigrant except by his land of birth, but San Francisco was not exempt from the national influx that brought great numbers of Jews to the United States in the years just before and just after the turn of the century.

A Ligurian sea captain, with his brother and son, is said to be the first Italian to settle in San Francisco. That was 1840. During the gold rush several hundred Genoese seamen came ashore. The census of 1850 identified 229 Italians in the state of California. The number increased slowly, then leaped sharply ahead in the years between 1900 and 1910. The early arrivals established truck gardens in the Bayview district and Visitacion Valley, and formed the first commission market in 1876. They brought with them, and introduced to the American housewife, the bell pepper, eggplant, artichokes, the herbs of their native land. Around the turn of the century, they began to operate their fishing boats from the foot of Vallejo Street. In time, the fishing fleet operating from Fishermen's Wharf, established nearby, became both a fixture and an important contributor to the city's scene.

The Irish, too, had been well represented among those who founded the city. Their numbers also showed a sharp increase—some 16,000 in 1900 had been born in their native Ireland; 60,000 San Franciscans had at least one parent who had been born on the "ould sod." The Irish found jobs in countless lines of endeavor, but they were especially prominent in the union movement that was struggling in 1900 to find a place in the sun.

Wages were good in 1900—at least according to the California Bureau of Labor Statistics: "A fact first and most pleasingly apparent is that, as regards wages, the wage-earner of California is, in almost every avocation, better paid than is the wage-earner in any other State in the Union."

Once again unions flourished, and not only among the skilled workers. Butchers and stablemen, hackmen and hod carriers, formed their own unions. Retail clerks obtained an agreement closing stores at six o'clock. Laundry workers sought shorter hours and increased pay. Beer bottlers and drivers, art glass blowers, ironworkers, milkers and milk wagon drivers, cloakmakers and picture frame workers, all joined the union parade—" a most varied collection of eggs . . . and some curious ducklings," snorted the paper of the skilled building tradesmen.

In the spring of 1901, influential employers raised a war chest to renew their fight against the unions. The membership of the new association was kept secret; it spoke only through its attorney, M. F. Michael. The Association promptly threw its weight into a series of labor disputes, helping to defeat the strikes and rout the new and untested unions.

A few months before, a handful of team drivers met one Saturday night to form a union. Among them were Michael Casey and John P. McLaughlin, who would lead the teamsters for the next four decades. An employer promptly fired several of his drivers for joining the union. By the next night, only five teamsters were left on the job. The company quickly signed a union contract. The short test of strength opened the way to a citywide contract between the teamsters' union and their employers, now organized into the Draymen's Association. The employers agreed they would hire only members of the union; it, in turn, promised that its members would work for nobody but members of the employers' association.

A showdown came innocently enough when a convention of the Epworth League, a Methodist Church organization, arrived in town. The League hired a nonunion firm to haul its baggage; it turned around and asked several union firms for help in handling it. Mike Casey announced that no union man would drive teams for the nonunion firm. Backed by the full strength of the citywide Employers Association, the draymen responded by firing every teamster who refused to handle League luggage. By July 24—a little more than a week since the employers' ultimatum—more than 1,300 had been fired. Next day, the union called the rest out on strike. It was, commented Father Peter Yorke, a close adviser of the teamster leaders, "an attempt of the rich men's union to disrupt the poor men's unions." The employers planted their feet: "The principle involved in this strike may be surrendered, but it cannot be compromised."

Farm hands from the valleys were brought in to take the strikers' place. Black men were imported and put to work. College students and discharged teamsters, just back from the Philippines, climbed up on the box. Police rode "shotgun" on the wagons, guiding the nonunion teamsters around town, often escorting them to lunch and home in the evening. Hoots and jeers gave way to fists and bricks. Strikers laid rough hands on the scabs; police were no more gentle in handling the teamsters.

Talk of a citywide general strike bubbled up. Union leaders turned to the one group that had the money, the experience, and the stability to carry on the fight. On July 29, the City Front Federation, representing the water-front unions, called out its 13,000 members in sympathy with the teamsters. Their strike left ships unloaded at the docks, stopped work on the Oakland water front and at the wheat warehouses at Crockett and Port Costa. Andrew Furuseth, the sailors' flinty leader, headed the joint strike committee. "There is no way of having peace," he told the sailors, "except by fighting for it."

As the city's economy slowed almost to a halt, violence grew. Strikebreakers were tracked down to saloons and boardinghouses. Some were virtually kidnaped and, with the help of friendly railroad crews, dumped into outgoing boxcars. The employers refused to budge. To complaints that wheat was rotting, they replied, "Let it rot." The stalemate held tight. In mid-August and again on Labor Day, thousands of union supporters turned out to parade impressively up Market Street. Soon after, though, the cooks and waiters gave up their four-month strike. Oakland longshoremen returned to work; once more, men began moving wheat at Crockett and Port Costa. But freight piled up on the San Francisco docks and scores of ships still swung idly at anchor in the bay.

On October 2, Governor Gage arrived in San Francisco,

quietly, without notice to unions or employers. He summoned union officials and leaders of the Draymen's Association. After a two-hour session, Governor Gage issued a simple, one-paragraph announcement that the "teamsters' strike and all collateral and sympathetic strikes or lockouts . . . are at an end." Neither the governor, the union leaders, nor the employers revealed how the truce had been reached, nor, then or afterward, the exact terms of the peace.

The teamsters lost their union shop; the other unions were badly mauled, losing members and draining their treasuries. In these ways, it was no union victory. But in union eyes, survival was victory. The employers had set out to weaken, if they could not destroy, the unions. No major purpose of the employers was accomplished and the Employers Association soon faded from the scene.

Years passed before the full impact of the battle could be measured. The unions grew stronger. San Francisco became known as a "union town" second to none. Organized labor maintained its dominance in local industrial relations for the next two decades.

Not the least of its repercussions, though, was the triumph of the Union Labor party in the city elections of 1901. It elected as mayor Eugene Schmitz, a handsome bassoon-player in a local theater orchestra. The party was in no real sense a labor party; most of the city's front-rank union leaders steered clear of it; unions had little voice in its policies. But its victory reflected the anger of San Francisco's working people, the strong feeling that the city administration had been less than neutral in the water-front battle. It also echoed their demand for a place in the city's sun.

Schmitz was re-elected in 1903, again in 1905. In the latter election he carried eighteen members of the Board of Supervisors into office with him. Under the guidance and manipulation of the party's political boss, a shrewd and scheming attorney, Abe Ruef, they began a systematic plundering of the city. They went into partnership with dishonest contractors, sold privileges and permits, extorted money from restaurant and saloon owners. They peddled franchises to corporations and took bribes from practically anybody who wanted a favor and was willing to pay for it.

When the extent of its graft began to come to the surface, investigation and prosecution soon followed. The graft prosecutions, though, yielded only years of public quarreling, violence and threats of violence, futile trials and election feuds. Interrupted briefly by the earthquake and fire of 1906, the prosecution succeeded in driving the culprits from office and the graft was mopped up. The Union Labor party was reorganized and returned briefly to power in 1910 under the leadership of P. H. McCarthy, the key figure in the hard-fisted building trades unions. After he was defeated for re-election as mayor in 1912, the party faded away.

The unions, in the long run, won the second battle. For the next twenty years they had it their way. But the war, even if laid aside, was not yet ended.

16 An "A-1" earthquake

James B. Stetson remembered being awakened by a heavy, jolting shock. The violent shaking nearly threw him out of bed and brought a large, glass-front bookcase crashing down. He rushed to the window, saw the street filled with a slowly rising white dust.

Kathryn Hulme remembered the quake throwing her against the wall. The earth seemed to "grumble," timber creaked, a crack opened in the wall. She watched the stairs wave and twist.

The great Italian tenor, Enrico Caruso, threw open his Palace Hotel window, bellowing what he later called the grandest notes he had ever sung. Only the night before he had sung *Carmen* to an enthusiastic and adoring audience beneath the Opera House's huge, gaslight chandelier, unique in the magnificence of its hand-cut crystal. Almost at the moment Caruso tested his voice from a hotel window, the great chandelier fell into the pit of the empty theater.

The quake was accompanied by "a noise like a broadside

from all the guns of hell." The cobblestones of Market Street seemed alive. Chimneys and spires snapped off, brick walls crumbled, buildings crashed. Fissures opened in the land and waves churned the earth. The first great shock stunned, staggered the few people on the streets. A second shock, ten seconds later, was even worse.

So, on Tuesday morning, April 18, 1906, at five-thirteen o'clock an earthquake struck San Francisco—not by any means its first but surely its worst.

San Francisco's first was recorded in 1808—its twenty-one shocks collapsed buildings at the Presidio, left great cracks in the walls of the commandante's house. In 1865, a quake caught Mark Twain strolling along Third Street. San Francisco had never seen, he commented, such destruction of mantel ornaments and toilet bottles. A minister, according to Twain, advised his flock to keep their seats. "There is no better place to die than this." After the third shock, he hastily added, "But outside is good enough." Bret Harte dismissed a little temblor in 1866 as "a rather good-humored affair." It lacked the "decided malevolence" of the 1865 quake. That, he said, "was a trespass with assault and battery superadded."

The 1906 quake, like its predecessors, was a product of the San Andreas fault. This great crack in the earth's crust comes in from the ocean near Point Arena, slices the Point Reyes peninsula from the mainland, touches land again at Mussel Rock. It slashes southeastward across the Coast Range and the southern end of the state, disappearing into the Gulf of California. In the 1906 quake, a sharp, sudden shift along the fault thrust the entire Point Reyes peninsula northwestward. A path leading to the front door of a nearby ranch house was shoved fifteen feet out of line.

San Francisco's Cliff House was three miles, the City Hall nine miles, from the fault trace. Author Gertrude Atherton asked the scientist George Davidson about the intensity of the 1906 quake. Seismologically, he thought it rated about 9, with 10 representing complete destruction. Then he added, "But I think A-1 would be a far better name for it."

On the far side of Van Ness Avenue, a housewife lighted her stove to prepare breakfast, not knowing that the gas mains had been ruptured. She started a fire that quickly swept through Hayes Valley. Soon scores of fires were re- ported—more fires than the city had fire engines. The city had 80 million gallons of water stored in reservoirs, but firemen coupling their hoses to the hydrants got only a thin trickle, then mud, then nothing. The quake had shattered the mains tapping the reservoirs, cracked the service pipes from cisterns. Dynamite became the major weapon in the desperate fight against the fire. By midday the blaze was out of control. The greater portion of the city east of Van Ness Avenue was on fire.

People, rich and poor, rushed from their homes, wear- ing whatever was close at hand and carrying the odd bits and pieces that represented, in that urgent moment, their most valued possessions. Some carried bird cages or hats, jewel boxes, cats. Some hauled their valuables to another, presumably safe site, only to have it overrun by the sweep- ing flames within hours. A telegraph operator tapped out a message at 9 A.M., saying he was leaving. "It's me for the simple life." More than three hours later, though, his in- struments were still clicking as he fed eastern stations re- ports. Finally, he clicked, he was packing and ready to run. A few more minutes, then simply, "Good-bye."

Mayor Schmitz asked the women of Los Angeles to bake bread and deliver it to the Chamber of Commerce to be rushed to the stricken city. Governor Pardee asked for "all available cooked food." President Theodore Roosevelt ordered the Navy to render all possible help. General Funston, without waiting for orders, called out the troops at the Presidio. Before the day was out, he had 1,500 soldiers on the streets. Western Union sent 5,000 messages to Los Angeles by train. One line carried official, outgoing messages. Southern Pacific offered to carry passengers away from the city without charge. In nine days it carried some 300,000 refugees.

Any saloons that were left were promptly closed and liquor supplies requisitioned. A sign went up identifying the burned-out remains of the not-quite-completed Fairmont Hotel. Next door another sign went up: "The Unfairmont."

The *Evening Daily News,* located out on Fourth Street, got out a single sheet, printed on one side, that afternoon. Its headline: "Hundreds Dead! Fire Follows Earthquake . . . City Seems Doomed for Lack of Water." Within minutes, a squad of soldiers sent the staff into the street and dynamited the building in an effort to block the fire's advance. The city's other newspapers, the *Examiner, Call,* and *Chronicle,* published a joint edition next morning on the *Oakland Tribune* presses.

Author Jack London sat for a time on Nob Hill watching the fire climb its slopes. Soon the flames swept over the hill, burning the Spreckels chateau, the Phelan mansion, the Hopkins castle. The Flood mansion alone survived.

The homeless made their way to parks and open areas.

Some carried blankets, a few provisions, a few possessions. John I. Walter wrote his parents traveling in Europe: "San Francisco . . . metropolis of the land of milk and honey, is going up in smoke." Antoine Borel, Jr., son of a wealthy Swiss banker, wrote: "Darling Papa & Mama & Sisters: A terrible thing has happened. San Francisco is no more."

That night, watchers in the Berkeley hills saw the whole eastern front of the city in flames against the night sky. At scattered points, a blaze flared upward, lighting the heavy clouds of smoke with a pink glow. When the sun rose next morning, its light was reddened by the smoke-filled air, casting a crimson hue over the waters of the bay.

Mayor Schmitz, already under heavy attack in the graft investigations, met the emergency with surprising strength. He summoned fifty leaders, including many of his political enemies, and formed them into a Relief Committee. His orders put the city under strict emergency discipline and initiated measures for dealing with the disaster. He cut off all gas and electricity, warned the citizens they could expect the city to remain in darkness until it was once again safe.

Work was started at once to house and feed the people of the city, even as help began flooding in from every part of the world. By Thursday morning distribution depots were set up outside the burned areas. Supplies from Army posts—milk, bread, other food—were passed out. Within days, clothing, blankets, tents, medicines, were being distributed.

Meanwhile squads of soldiers dynamited buildings, opening great, yawning gaps in an effort to halt the spreading flames. Time after time, the blaze leaped the gaps, forcing the fire fighters back to new lines of defense. Finally, slowed by a shifting wind, the fire turned back on itself and burned out. Sunday morning, April 23, Mayor Schmitz announced the fire was under control.

San Franciscans set up housekeeping in tents or shacks in parks or vacant lots. In the next two months, more than eight thousand refugee houses and barracks were run up and occupied. Many stayed in use for several years. For six weeks all cooking was done outdoors until chimneys and gas and electrical connections were inspected. Business firms reopened in private houses, many of them along Van Ness Avenue, outside the burned-out area.

A. P. Hotaling & Co. announced that its stock of whiskey, two thousand barrels, had survived and was on sale. Commented Charles K. Field:

> *If, as they say, God spanked the town*
> *For being over-frisky—*
> *Why did He burn the churches down*
> *And spare Hotaling's whisky?*

Bancroft-Whitney, publishers of law books, cancelled $30,000 owed it by San Francisco lawyers. "Lawyers outside of San Francisco," the firm said, "can help out by remitting at once amounts due." The San Francisco Real Estate Board thought it better to speak of "the great fire" rather than "the great earthquake." On Market Street, somebody suggested every man passing by should be asked to put in twenty minutes shoveling debris. The street was soon cleared for traffic.

Well-constructed buildings, it turned out, were hardly damaged. Poor construction fell victim to the quake; frame constructions—San Francisco was 90 per cent frame—toppled on countless victims, burst into flames. In all, 512 blocks holding 28,188 buildings were demolished in seventy-two hours. Damage by the quake was estimated at some 20 million dollars; by the fire, more than 400 million. In the Presidio, Golden Gate Park, in parks and lots scattered around the city, a quarter of a million people were encamped; a hundred thousand more, perhaps, had left town.

Will Irwin, a newspaper man with San Francisco roots, wrote of "The City That Was": "The old San Francisco is dead. The gayest, lightest hearted, most pleasure loving city of the western continent . . . is a horde of refugees living among ruins. It may rebuild; it probably will . . . it can never be the same."

Rhymed Lawrence W. Harris: "From the Ferries to Van Ness you're a Godforsaken mess, but the damnedest finest ruins—nothing more or nothing less."

Monica Sutherland years later compared the trials of San Franciscans to those of Londoners under the bombings of World War II. "One common denominator exists: the shining courage of ordinary people confronted by extraordinary perils."

A famous reporter, Ray Stannard Baker, noted: "For an instant there were neither millionaires nor paupers—just American people."

San Francisco began to rebuild even before the ashes cooled. Three years after the fire, buildings worth 150 million dollars were erected. Of the more than 28,000 buildings destroyed, more than 20,000 were replaced by the end of the third year. There was hardly a minute, day or night, in those years when the sounds of riveting could not be heard.

17   The battle resumed

For some ten years after the quake and fire, San Francisco enjoyed—or endured—the reputation of being the nation's No. 1 union town. Union-negotiated rules set the wages and hours and job conditions for tens of thousands of workers in every manner of industry. The building trades unions, especially, imposed their demanding and sometimes rigid code on the construction industry. The employers, though, made it abundantly clear that they were not happy with this state of affairs.

Then, on June 1, 1916, the longshoremen struck. The dockers claimed they needed a wage increase to make up for higher prices, rising under the pressure of war in Europe. The employers charged that they were violating their contract and replaced them with strikebreakers. On June 9, the longshoremen went back to work. Both strikebreakers and union men were mauled and beaten, and some were killed. The employers refused to withdraw the armed guards and strikebreakers on the docks. The longshoremen walked out a second time.

The Chamber of Commerce summoned the city's businessmen to an emergency meeting. Some two thousand, they claimed, turned out. The Chamber angrily declared it would maintain at any cost the right of employers to hire "union men or nonunion in whole or in part." The unions read the Chamber pronouncement as a declaration of war. Captain Robert Dollar, head of one of the port's great steamship companies, urged the employers to send two strikers to the hospital for every strikebreaker injured in the dock war. Frederick J. Koster, a barrel manufacturer who was president of the Chamber, headed a Law and Order Committee pledged to carry out the Chamber's open-shop campaign. Before it was minutes old, the Committee claimed pledges of support totaling more than $200,000; the amount would soar to a million dollars, "in round figures," before the end of the year.

Although the longshoremen ended their second strike on July 17, the businessmen pushed ahead with their plans. They now focused on the Preparedness Day parade scheduled to take place just five days later—on July 22. Similar parades in New York and Washington had called on the nation to prepare for the war already raging in Europe. In San Francisco, Preparedness Day took on a somewhat different color. With the Chamber guiding it behind-the-scenes, the parade would be an open-shop demonstration wrapped in patriotic banners.

The unions were strongly suspicious of the parade's sponsors and just as strongly opposed to "the fostering of the war spirit." The San Francisco Labor Council called on its members to "make no other protest than . . . silent nonparticipation." In that way any possibility that a violent disturbance of the parade could be blamed on the unions would be forestalled.

The parade was late in starting but at 1:31 P.M., out stepped Mayor "Sunny Jim" Rolph, wearing gold-heeled cowboy boots and waving a white ten-gallon cowboy hat, a perky flower in the buttonhole of his frock coat. Marching units moved from the side streets into the Market Street line of march. At 2:04 the Grand Army of the Republic, veterans of the Civil War, began moving out of Steuart Street. At six minutes after two o'clock, at that point, there was a sudden, shattering roar, a sharp, stunning explosion. It killed ten bystanders, wounded some forty.

Four days later the Law and Order Committee convened a meeting in the Civic Auditorium to mourn those who had died in the bombing.

"They sat with us last night at the Auditorium, the brooding shades of the Vigilantes," a San Francisco reporter, who was also the publicity director of the Law and Order Committee, wrote. "Grim, stern, patriotic, the sons of the sires of 1856 pledged themselves to carry on."

Back of the Committee's activities, union leaders felt, was the unspoken but unmistakable intent to make the bombing a symbol of "labor violence." That intent took shape in what has been called "one of the most highly publicized antilabor campaigns ever conducted."

Police arrested Warren Billings, Israel Weinberg, and Edward D. Nolan for the crime, and announced they were seeking Tom Mooney and his wife, Rena. On July 27, the Mooneys were arrested while on their way back to San Francisco from a Russian River vacation to turn themselves in. The choice of these five—and especially of Mooney and

Billings—fitted with tailored precision into the pattern of war preparations and of the employers' anti-union campaign. Billings had once been jailed for possession of dynamite. Mooney had been tried and acquitted on a similar charge. Both were known as radicals; both had won the enmity of open-shop employers by their activities in strikes and organizing campaigns.

Mooney and Billings were convicted; the others were freed. Mooney was sentenced to death, Billings to life imprisonment. No effort was made, a U.S. government factfinding commission reported years later, to discover the actual perpetrators of the crime. The police, the commission said, merely conducted "a hunt for evidence to convict the arrested defendants." The evidence was supplied by witnesses described as a prostitute, a drug addict, a psychopathic liar, a woman suffering from hallucinations. "We must have been slightly crazed by the hysteria of the time," the trial judge commented later.

Fremont Older, the celebrated San Francisco editor who fought years to vindicate the two prisoners, declared that, when all was known, it would be clear that the state conspired "to murder a man with the instruments that the people have provided for bringing about justice. There isn't a scrap of testimony . . . that wasn't perjured, except that of the man who drew the blueprints of Market Street."

A swelling protest, heard halfway around the world, saved Mooney from death. Numerous investigations and repeated exposure of the flimsy and often fraudulent case against the two men, though, failed to win their release. The campaign for vindication continued over more than twenty years. In 1938, Governor Culbert Olson finally freed them.

That summer of violence in 1916 set the stage for the
Law and Order Committee's successful effort to restrict
picketing by law. "There is no such thing as peaceful picketing," Chamber of Commerce President Koster cried. "It is
un-American. It hurts the city." The Committee put four
hundred girls to work phoning every voter who had a phone,
urging them to vote for the ordinance. Most of them did.

In the fall of 1919, the longshoremen struck again. The
employers blamed a "radical element" in the union and refused to have anything to do with it. After four months,
they signed a contract with a new union—the so-called
"Blue Book" union. Probably, an employer representative
admitted later, it was inspired by the employers. Soon after,
as the country was pinned down by a short, sharp depression, the shipowners broke the unions of the officers and
men who sailed the nation's merchant ships.

The year before, San Francisco's building contractors had
allied themselves with the Chamber of Commerce to seek a
showdown with the building trades unions. When the unions
refused to accept a 7½ per cent pay cut, the builders and
the Chamber locked out the men. To be rehired, a man was
forced to tear up his union card. Employers said they would
hire both union and nonunion men under what they called
the "American Plan." In practice, it turned out to be nonunion, rather than union, men who got the jobs. The Industrial Association, the employer organization, recruited and
trained nonunion workers.

The Industrial Association showed the way in eliminating
unions in scores of other industries. And the city's bankers
and businessmen sponsored a permit system under which
supplies and credit were withheld from any employer agree-

ing to deal with a union. As a result of the employer campaign, San Francisco became an open-shop town—as anti-union as it had once been union. In 1930, an employer spokesman wrote, "Today organized labor still functions in San Francisco, but its irresponsible power is broken. . . . The city is free." "It was a debacle indeed," said a reporter. The unions "made a single dizzy plunge from the loftiest heights to the lowest and darkest depths."

The harsh realities of industrial life played a grim counterpoint to the light and occasionally fantastic themes sounded in other aspects of San Francisco life. One legend was flung into the air on Christmas Eve in 1910 when the great opera star, Luisa Tetrazzini, gave an open-air concert at Kearny and Market Streets. A green flare, then a searchlight and a fanfare of trumpets, presented the singer to the throng. Silently, in near darkness, they listened as she sang "The Last Rose of Summer" and "Auld Lang Syne."

In 1915, to celebrate completion of the Panama Canal, the city threw a great party—the Panama Pacific International Exposition. She hauled up tons of sand from the bay bottom, filled in a 635-acre site east of old Fort Point. The Exposition held forth in architecturally-striking buildings, bathed in an impressive aura of electric light. It brought celebrated artists of every kind to the city—perhaps none more appropriate than Lotta Crabtree. As a young and lovely red-haired dancer she had been showered with gold by the Forty-niners in the diggings and at famous San Francisco resorts, such as the What Cheer, The Willows, Bella Union. Now sixty-eight, she returned for an "open-air jubilation" at the iron fountain that she had given the city and that still stands at Kearny and Market, where, a few years before, Tetrazzini had sung. The streets were jammed and the crowds cheered Lotta's songs.

Since the 1850's the collection of saloons, houses of prostitution, and disreputable boardinghouses centering around lower Pacific Street had been known far and wide as the Barbary Coast. Deserted during the day, the area filled at night with gamblers, prostitutes, and confidence men offering their special pastimes to visitors and residents alike.

Women associated with the YWCA and several charity organizations set out in 1913 to rescue the women who were caught in the Barbary Coast's vice. Of five hundred women sought out in the uplift campaign, ten accepted help, only one took a job. At least one of the girls said that if she sold nothing more than soft drinks, she would still earn more than respectable jobs paid. The police, however, a few years later, wiped out the district and Barbary Coast joined the legends of the city's past. Today it is a smartly refurbished and decorated haven for wholesale furniture and fabric houses.

The city, too, reached out into the sand hills to the west. Gertrude Atherton, novelist and occasional historian of her native California, found the new neighborhoods depressing. "I used to walk past those long rows of houses, drab, with bow windows, as alike as a row of lead pencils in a box . . . despite the sentimentalists, it was gray and ugly and depressing." In the Western Addition and Pacific Heights, few such houses are left now. High-rise, high-priced apartment houses and still handsome mansions replaced many of them. The bow or bay windows, incidentally, were a San Francisco device, some said, to capture maximum light despite the city's deep and narrow building lots.

The city's literary tradition was in good health in the first two decades of the century. Jack London graduated from an Oakland cannery, raided the Oakland oyster beds with gangs of local "pirates," joined the new gold rush to the Klondike. From these experiences he fashioned his well-known tales of adventure, as well as lesser-known books expounding his radical philosophy.

Cincinnatus Heine Miller, a grandiloquent poet of the West, dropped his first names in favor of Joaquin, a bow to the notorious California bandit Joaquin Murietta. He won his first fame in London with his western-style clothes as well as his poems.

Perhaps the poet who came closest to symbolizing San Francisco's "Bohemians" was George Sterling, who lived a long affair with his "cool, grey city of love." Sterling came west in 1890 to work in a real estate office. A gay eccentric, he once plunged into a Golden Gate Park lake to pluck a water lily for a lady. He was moody, brooding, changeable. He enjoyed boxing, boasted of his ability to outswim and outwalk any man; he hated dominoes and wrote gentle lines of verse:

> *At the end of our streets is sunrise;*
> *At the end of our streets are spars;*
> *At the end of our streets is sunset;*
> *At the end of our street are stars.*

Sterling spent hours at Poppa Coppa's famous restaurant, hangout for the literary and artistic set, drinking a mixture of whiskey, warm water, and sugar. All his drinking, though, could not still the sharp pain that tortured him—"like a pencil boring into him," he said. The poison he swallowed did.

A literary light of a different character was Fremont Older. He had set type for a variety of gold field newspapers before becoming a reporter for, and later editor of the *Bulletin*. Older pioneered in publishing sensational personal confessions and inside stories. He launched a war against Abe Ruef and his grafting associates in City Hall and the Union Labor party. Older was a principal figure in raising the money that financed the investigation and prosecution of graft and corruption. Having helped convict Ruef, though, Older then campaigned for a pardon for him. He felt that Ruef had been only an agent of bigger men who had gone free.

Older protested capital punishment, befriended scores of ex-convicts. He was suspicious at first of Tom Mooney and Warren Billings. Then, as evidence piled up that the trial evidence had been perjured, that their conviction was the result of a frame-up, he became a vigorous, stubborn proponent of freedom for the two men. He exposed the frame-up and perjured evidence in countless columns in the *Bulletin*. When Publisher Loring Pickering ordered the Mooney case dropped, Older jumped to William Randolph Hearst's *Call*. At Hearst's invitation, he brought the Mooney case with him.

Ironically, eleven years later, what was left of his old *Bulletin* was merged with the *Call*. The indomitable Older became the editor of the merged papers.

18   The last battle?

For sheer size and reach, the great depression went far beyond any economic slump the nation had ever known. More
than fifteen million men were out of work when Franklin
D. Roosevelt took the oath of office in March, 1933. They
had been jobless, not for days or for weeks, but for month
after month and, in millions of cases, year after year.

In San Francisco, too. Bread lines and soup kitchens provided meager meals for the homeless unemployed. Families
of the unemployed were sustained by relief payments—from
private charity until the load became too great, then from
the city and state and, finally, from the Federal government.
Thousands scrambled for what work there was. Down on
the water front men bribed straw bosses with a bottle of
whiskey or a few bucks in return for a few days' work. Men
sailed deepwater ships out of the port for as little as $25 a
month. Uptown, wages were cut repeatedly, hours stretched
out, conditions deteriorated.

The consequences of years of joblessness were assessed

in November, 1932, by the California Unemployment Commission, a panel of leading citizens appointed by Governor James Rolph. "Unemployment and loss of income have ravaged numerous homes," its report declared. "It has broken the spirits of their members, undermined their health, robbed them of self-respect, destroyed their efficiency and employability." It added: "There is no security, no foothold, no future to sustain them. Savings are depleted, and debts mount. . . . Woman and child labor further undermine the stability of the home. . . . Food rations are pared down, rents go unpaid, families are evicted. They must uproot their households frequently. Physical privations undermine body and heart. The peace and harmony of the home vanish."

Men and boys took to the road, grabbing meals from a convenient bread line, sleeping in a flophouse. Others took up residence in mushrooming towns of the jobless. "Hoovervilles" they were called, built from packing boxes, sheets of tin, scrap lumber.

Franklin D. Roosevelt's unforgettable inaugural address on March 4, 1933, echoed the people's desperate hopes from the steps of the Capitol. Soon, from Washington came a rushing, tumbling stream of programs, aimed at returning the jobless to work, restoring profits to business, repairing the damage of four years of economic disaster.

In that first early flush of hope, the longshoremen on the San Francisco water front rebelled. They revolted against the star gang system that gave the cream of the work to a favored few and distributed the leftovers among the unfavored many. They protested the hiring system that required them to "shape up" on the docks every morning, rain or shine, while callous and often dishonest bosses handed out the day's work. They echoed the anger of thousands with part-time work or no work at all, with long hours and low pay, with miserly relief handouts—most of all, perhaps, with the humiliating indignity of unemployment.

Not the least of all, the longshoremen revolted against the "Blue Book" union that had been sponsored, protected, and maintained by their employers for fourteen years. In 1933, the National Industrial Recovery Act said, for the first time in the nation's history, that workers had a right to join a union and bargain collectively. Thousands of dockers deserted the old, employer-dominated union and joined the International Longshoremen's Association, a union chartered by the American Federation of Labor. But efforts to negotiate an agreement with the water-front employers ended in stalemate. Neither President Roosevelt nor a fact-finding commission could find an acceptable answer or stave off a strike.

On the morning of May 9, 1934, the longshoremen walked out—at Portland and San Pedro and Seattle as well as at San Francisco—"for better conditions, a shorter day, and a living wage," they said. Employers' ads declared, "It is an ill-advised strike. Be reasonable." They advertised for men to work on the docks behind the picket lines. As rapidly as ships tied up in port, sailors and firemen and stewards, the engineers, mates, and often the masters joined the strike. They, too, demanded recognition for their unions along with better pay and conditions.

Joseph P. Ryan, national president of the I.L.A., flew out to San Francisco in an effort to settle the strike. Twice he arranged settlements; twice the strikers rejected them. With Ryan discredited, control of the strike shifted to a rank-and-

file strike committee, headed by a onetime Australian seaman, Harry Bridges. He had quit the sea in 1922 to work on
the docks. Soon he had established himself as a skilled longshoreman and won a place in a star gang. He had joined an
unsuccessful effort to revive the union in 1924, was active
in the successful attempt in 1933. Around him in the decades ahead would swirl angry controversy, yielding finally in
later years to a place as an "elder statesman" of the water
front. But in 1934, he was chosen to head the local strike
committee and, in turn, the joint strike committee speaking
for all the striking unions.

The teamsters initially had voted to stay away from the
docks. Then they declared they would not haul any cargo
handled by strikebreakers. Their action crippled the water
front. The employers were faced with a choice between set-
tling the strike or hauling the freight themselves. They chose
the latter. The employer-sponsored Industrial Association
rented warehouses, purchased trucks, prepared to open the
port. After several delays, they set the date for July 3.

"Stay away from the water front," Chief of Police Quinn
warned the public. The police force will have its hands full,
he said; it didn't want to harm any innocent bystanders. He
added two hundred men to the force, laid in supplies of tear
gas and riot guns.

Early on the morning of July 3 pickets gathered at Pier
38. Patrol cars and sidetracked freight cars cut off traffic
from the area. At 1:27 P.M. the steel doors on the docks
lifted. Eight patrol cars emerged, followed by five lumbering
freight trucks. Pickets surged forward and police responded
with tear gas. Mounted officers swung their clubs at pickets'
heads; the pickets fired back with bricks and stones and fists.

All through the afternoon the police and pickets fought. The heavily guarded trucks made eighteen trips between the docks and the warehouse; then they rested. On the next day, the Fourth of July, the Industrial Association declared the port was open. A tense holiday stillness hung over the city.

Early on July 5—the day came to be known as Bloody Thursday—fighting resumed. Along the Embarcadero, up and down Rincon Hill, police charged the pickets, and the pickets replied with bricks and rocks. Police met them with gas and gunfire. Not one battle raged, the *Chronicle* reported, but a hundred, big and little. Pickets drifted back toward I.L.A. headquarters on Steuart Street. Near Mission Street, police fired riot guns into a crowd. Two men died: Howard Sperry, a longshoreman, and Nick Bordoise, a cook. Strikers chalked a clumsy memorial on the spot where they had fallen. "POLICE MURDER," the memorial said. That afternoon, Governor Merriam ordered the National Guard into the city. By nightfall, soldiers patrolled the docks, their machine guns ominously emplaced atop the piers.

Four days later, in stunning silence, the longshoremen, seafaring strikers, their families and friends, men, women, children, paraded up Market Street. A truck bore the bodies of the two dead men. No police patrolled the solemn march; men in the black jeans and white caps of the longshoremen quietly directed the flow of the mourners. The quiet shuffle of marching feet underscored the bitter, angry silence. "A stupendous and reverent procession," one reporter wrote, "that astounded the city."

A citywide union committee was named to consider a general strike. But union after union voted to strike without waiting for the committee's decision. The teamsters met and voted to walk out. Mike Casey, the now white-haired giant of a man who had led them in the angry battle of 1901, warned them they could lose everything—their strike benefits, their union contract, their union charter. "Nothing could have prevented that vote," he said later. "In all my thirty years of leading these men, I have never seen them so determined."

On the morning of July 16, the general strike began. Commuters emerged from the Ferry building to see an empty Market Street. Its four-abreast streetcar tracks were empty as far as the eye could see. Trucks, jitneys, and cabs disappeared from the streets. Markets quickly sold out their stocks and closed their doors. Service stations closed. Liquor stores and saloons were shuttered. Just nineteen restaurants remained open. All this "By order of the General Strike Committee." Outraged editorials and civic leaders screamed "revolution."

A new kind of violence erupted. Vigilante committees— 1934-style—quickly, almost mysteriously formed and raided the headquarters and meeting halls of radical and so-called "radical" groups. They echoed the charges that the employers and the newspapers had been shouting since the strike began; the strike was in the hands of radicals, they claimed. They charged leaders with fomenting strife instead of working for settlement. The "communist agitators" should be replaced by "American" leaders, they said.

The raiders were frequently followed by carloads of police who arrested the beaten and stunned victims of the raids. The Marine Workers Industrial Union, the Communist party, and *Western Worker* headquarters were among those raided. Hundreds were arrested. "Are you a communist?"

one man was asked. "Hell, no," came the reply. "I'm a Baptist." One city judge, regaining his senses, said that the raiders had acted "like a pack of mad wolves." The record was filled with unlawful arrests, unlawful searches and seizures, excessive bail, unfair trials, the denial of counsel, deportation of workers, and, a study of law enforcement said, "other violations of the fundamental rights of American citizens."

More restaurants were opened on the second day of the strike, some restrictions eased. Streetcarmen, threatened with the loss of civil service pensions, returned to work. Restrictions were further loosened the next day; on the fourth day, the General Strike Committee voted to end the strike. The point had been made. Water-front employers and longshoremen, shipowners and seafarers' unions, submitted their disputes to an arbitration board.

The water-front strike inspired workers in every kind of job to organize. Department store and "five-and-dime" store clerks formed a union. Workers organized in warehouses and machine shops and foundries. The building trades threw off the yoke of the American Plan and the Industrial Association, sponsors of the hated open shop. Unionism spread to public employees, carmen, restaurant and hotel workers. Strikes broke out in department stores, warehouses, hotels. Union membership more than doubled between 1933 and 1940.

For fifteen years the fight for power on the docks and on the ships raged. It was nearly that long, too, before the organized employers generally seemed ready to concede that the unions were there to stay. Since then, employers and unions have fought repeatedly over wages or hours or benefits, but the right of the unions to live and function no longer

seems to be seriously questioned in San Francisco. They
have built a solid structure of labor-management relations
and achieved a high level of industrial peace. In the sense
that this day-to-day working relationship is built into the
city's economic life, San Francisco is a union town again.

19 Two faces of war

Sunday, December 7, 1941, was clear, cool, the sun bright, the air relaxed and soft like an autumn day. A few sailboats glided over the sun-streaked waters of the bay. Many San Franciscans, lazing over a late Sunday breakfast, skimming the Sunday papers, radios chattering in the background, barely heard the first brief one-line bulletins that were read just before noon. Honolulu and Manila were being bombed, the cryptic reports said.

Suddenly the radio programs were shattered by repeated, blood-chilling announcements: "Attention all officers and men, Twelfth Naval District and Alameda Naval Air Station: Report to your stations immediately." Similar messages rolled out in tense, controlled tones for members of army units, fire and police, coast defense units. The first newspapers hit the streets about two o'clock, the *Chronicle's* front page screaming "WAR" in four-inch letters. Newsboys bootjacked the papers in the residential districts, their hoarse shouts bouncing off the Sunday-quiet houses.

The first reaction was a stunned surprise. Then indignation, anger. Mayor Angelo Rossi declared a state of emergency. Recruiting for the city's civil defense forces, lagging until then, suddenly spurted. Long lines of volunteers, anxious to sign up as air raid wardens, auxiliary firemen and police, formed at fire and police stations all over town.

Weekenders returning to the city that night, some still unaware of the day's events, were puzzled to find the Golden Gate Bridge blacked out. (It proved to be a mistake; later the bridge lights came on again.) The Presidio next door was lighted, though, and bustling. The lights of the San Francisco–Oakland Bay Bridge sparkled on the dark waters of the bay, but soldiers now patrolled its ramps and along the Embarcadero.

Shrieking fire sirens shattered the quiet of the next night. Police and air raid wardens, new at the job, pounded on doors, demanding residents pull their blinds, turn off their lights. Fourth Interceptor Command had picked up "unidentified enemy" planes 100 miles due west. Radio stations clicked off. Street lights blinked out. Still, a great sign atop a finance firm spelled out "SAFE." And lighted store windows specked the city's main streets. "From Twin Peaks, 'blacked-out' San Francisco sparkled like New Orleans at Mardi Gras time," the *Chronicle* reported.

Three more warnings were issued during the night to silent radios and doused-out lights. Next day, the War Department said it knew nothing of the raid, but Lieutenant General John L. DeWitt, commander of the Fourth Army, insisted, "Last night there were planes over this community! They were enemy planes. I mean Japanese planes. . . . Bombing is bound to come." The mayor, chided by reporters on the great gaps of light in the city's blackout, responded huffily, "Well, no bombs fell."

Some of the tension of those early hours of war focused inevitably on the city's Japanese community. The attack on Pearl Harbor, after nearly half a century, breathed life into Hearst's "Yellow Peril." The sensational Sunday-supplement predictions of a war of the races suddenly seemed to come true. Years of anti-Oriental, anti-Japanese agitation found a shattering justification. "It was like a rubber band breaking, a rubber band which had been stretched out for a long time," a special officer on Market Street told a reporter that night. "Ever since I was a kid, we've been expecting something like this. Now it's come and it's a good thing and I think almost everybody thinks so."

Agents of the Federal Bureau of Investigation swiftly arrested "certain" marked Japanese aliens. Chief of Police Charles Dullea dispatched a special detail of uniformed men to supplement the four officers who normally patrolled the Japanese neighborhood. The policemen were told to expect anything. They found windows blacked out in most of the houses. Some of the stores—the Oriental curio shops, the sukiyaki and tempura restaurants, the papa-mama grocery stores—remained open. Few Japanese ventured out on the streets. Traffic thickened as curiosity seekers nosed around to see what was going on. The police spent most of their time nudging the sightseers along.

Japanese had been relative latecomers to California. The census had counted only 55 in 1870. By 1900, the number had climbed to 24,000. Ten years later, it had multiplied nearly three times. Japanese had replaced the Chinese, driven off by anti-Chinese riots, on the great valley's farms.

But they, too, fell victim to the same race hatred. In 1906 the San Francisco school board announced plans to segregate Oriental youngsters. The decision precipitated an international dispute. President Theodore Roosevelt himself intervened with the school board in an effort to reverse the decision. Soon after, though, the Gentlemen's Agreement with Japan barred all Japanese laborers from the United States, except those going to join close relatives.

Japanese farm workers, as soon as they were able, had bought or rented land to work on their own. In 1913 the Alien Land Law, aimed at the land-owning Japanese, prohibited aliens from acquiring land. Despite appeals from President Woodrow Wilson the law was stiffened in 1920. The agitation against the Orientals was quieted, but by no means stilled. The American Legion, the State Grange, the Native Sons, the State Federation of Labor, among others, continued the anti-Oriental campaign. With the outbreak of war, the agitation was quickly renewed.

Talk of evacuating the Japanese from the west coast welled up almost at once. There were at the time 127,000 Japanese in the three coastal states, 80 per cent of them in California. San Francisco was the home of slightly more than 5,000. Four days after the attack on Pearl Harbor the coast was declared a theater of war—reason enough, their antagonists said, for ousting the Japanese. Many, including pundit Walter Lippmann, feared the Pacific Coast was in danger of attack "from within and from without."

Japanese credits were frozen, Japanese-owned banks taken over. Some Japanese could not meet their payrolls. Some could not even buy groceries. At first, Japanese-Americans were encouraged to leave the area voluntarily, but they faced an uncertain welcome in other parts of the land. In the Midwest, where a Japanese face was a rarity, signs cropped up, "Japs not wanted," "Japs not welcome." They were refused service in restaurants, hotels, service stations.

On February 13, 1942, the west coast delegation in Congress recommended to the President "immediate evacuation of all persons of Japanese lineage." The Congressmen were not alone. Many—public officials and private citizens, individually and in organized groups—joined in the cry for evacuation. They argued, as did then Attorney General Earl Warren (later Chief Justice of the United States Supreme Court), that the Japanese were a potential danger to the nation. Both the American-born and the Japanese-born, they claimed, menaced the national security with the threat of espionage and sabotage.

Under authority of President Roosevelt, the Army promptly removed "enemy aliens" from designated zones— harbors, airports, near power lines. Congressman John Tolan of Oakland opened Congressional committee hearings on the question on February 21 in San Francisco, though the decision to remove the Japanese probably had already been made.

Starting in March, in a series of 108 separate orders, General DeWitt ordered all Japanese, aliens and citizens alike, young and old, men, women, and children, evacuated from California, Oregon, and Washington. By June some hundred thousand people had been corralled in hastily converted assembly centers. By November, they were behind barbed wire. What were called, politely, relocation centers were scattered in remote areas of Utah, Arizona, California, Idaho, Wyoming, Colorado, Arkansas.

"We have to be tough, even if civil rights do take a beating for a time," the *Chronicle* claimed. "Justified, if not just," the military declared.

"Military necessity" supplied the justification; the west coast was in danger of invasion and threatened by sabotage and espionage, the military claimed. No known acts of either had occurred, but this was interpreted to mean merely that the enemy was awaiting the right moment. Evacuation was necessary, proponents argued, to protect the Japanese themselves against mob violence. But the proponents relied chiefly on the simple fact that the Japanese, neither the foreign-born nor the American-born, had ever really become a part of American society. The Japanese were seen, as the Chinese had been seen before them, as a tightly-knit racial group, bound by ties of language, religion, and customs. General DeWitt contended that the Japanese race is "an enemy race." Its racial heritage was undiluted, the general claimed, though they were second- and third-generation, born on American soil, citizens by right, Americanized. There is no way to determine their loyalty, he insisted. "Theoretically, he is still a Japanese and you can't change him . . . by giving him a piece of paper."

Families were uprooted, businesses and farms and household goods were sold at incredible sacrifice. In San Francisco, the little shops, the homes and buildings around Sutter and Buchanan Streets, were shuttered. Education was broken off. Japanese holdings worth some 400 million dollars were sacrificed at tiny fractions of their value or put under often careless and indifferent custody. After the war the United States government returned about ten cents on the dollar to the victims of the evacuation.

Early in 1943, a Japanese-American combat team was recruited, drawing men from behind the wires of the concentration camps. The army sought 2,500; more than 10,000 volunteered. The 100th Infantry Battalion and the 442nd Regimental Combat Teams proved probably as valiant and effective fighters as any in the European theater of war. They fought in seven major campaigns. Official Army records said casualties were three times the unit's official strength. They won repeated unit citations and 18,143 individual decorations. Ironically, posthumous decorations were awarded families of the dead heroes behind the barbed wire of relocation centers, under the watch of machine guns and searchlight towers. Other Japanese-Americans served valiantly in the Pacific and Asiatic theaters of war and in other services of the nation at war.

The evacuation of the Japanese was neither right nor necessary. The losses they suffered from hardship, mental anguish, loss of employment, earnings or business profits, were irreparable. And the injustice they encountered was immeasurable. They were charged essentially with being of Japanese descent, denied any opportunity to face their accusers, to present witnesses of their own, to have their day in court.

Even as the Japanese were being rooted out of their homes, the advance guard of a new army of immigrants was reaching San Francisco. They were, in good part, black-skinned. They came mainly from the farms and small towns of the South and Southwest, though a sizable number were from the ghettos of big, industrial cities.

War industries, the Bay Area shipyards particularly, were

reaching out to new, previously untouched masses of un-skilled workers. They included, according to Kathryn Archi-bald, a sociologist turned shipyard worker, the drifters and the failures, farmworkers living on the edge of subsistence, women who in peacetime could expect only casual and poorly paid work, blacks cramped by prejudice and ham-pered by ignorance.

San Francisco before World War II had a black popula-tion of about five thousand, only slightly less than the Jap-anese with whom they shared a ghetto lying in and about the Western Addition and centered on Fillmore Street. In the next few years the black population multiplied two to four times. What happened to Willie Stokes, as sociologist Cy W. Record reported it, offers some insight into what happened to many of those newcomers.

In June, 1941, 27-year-old Willie Stokes lived on a cot-ton plantation in Arkansas. He worked each day from dawn to dusk—from "can to can't" see. For each day he was given a credit at the plantation store of $1.25. He was also given a small plot of land for a kitchen garden, a two-room window-less shack to house his wife and two children. Shipyards and war plants, along with stories of high pay and steady work, beckoned loudly and clearly. Stokes joined the wartime exodus to San Francisco.

In June, 1943, Willie Stokes was working as a welder in the Kaiser shipbuilding yard No. 2 in Richmond, a small industrial suburb of San Francisco. He was paid $10 for an eight-hour workday. He may have lived in wartime housing somewhere around the bay or crowded into the black neigh-borhoods in San Francisco's Fillmore district, in west Oak-land or south Berkeley. Thousands of Afro-Americans found jobs in the shipyards and in many other Bay Area industries and—even more important—at levels of skill and pay that few of them had ever before experienced.

Poor whites were pouring into California cities, too. "Okie" was the label pinned on white newcomers from Oklahoma. Soon it stretched to strangers from Arkansas, Texas, the Southwest. Soon, too, it came to describe any newcomer who was "uncitified, unskilled, accustomed to a low standard of living and who threatened the economic security of the older residents."

Many of the so-called "Okies" had come west during the years of depression and the Great Drouth in the thirties. They had found jobs planting and harvesting the crops of the Great Central Valley. As they grew accustomed to their new homes and business improved, they moved into the small towns and into industrial jobs. They, like the blacks, responded readily to the call for help in the mushrooming shipyards and war plants. Many other poor whites, fresh from the farms of the Southwest, joined the earlier arrivals there.

The shipyards seethed with antagonisms born out of the clash of cultures. Barred at first, the blacks were then hired for unskilled work as the demand for man (and woman) power grew increasingly urgent. They cleaned up after the more skilled crafts, worked at the less demanding jobs. In time, though, they found their way into most of the major trades and to rising levels of skill. They apparently worked at countless tasks with white workers, but the prejudice against them was still there, just barely under the surface. The black was the butt of countless gestures and remarks. He was referred to as "jigaboo" and "jungle bunny." Often the best that was offered was, "They're okay as long as they keep their place."

Other groups were also the butt of shipyard prejudice. Portuguese were sometimes called "streamlined niggers." It was fashionable to hate Japanese. Chinese were accepted with little dislike but with little friendliness. American Indians were respected, even admired, though; Okies often boasted of any trace of Cherokee blood. Jews were seen through the eyes of prejudice: money-grubbers, loan sharks, clever. Women, too, were resented, though in time accepted. Manners improved, one woman noted, and language was cleaned up; still the feeling persisted that a shipyard was no place for a woman.

Mushrooming work forces in the shipyards boosted union membership beyond any the unions had ever known. But skilled craftsmen were reluctant to see their skills watered down or broken into a few, repetitive tasks. It seemed to threaten the very skills that gave them pride and status. Their reluctance was reflected in a failure to encourage newcomers to take part in union affairs. The craftsmen sometimes even imposed limitations on the newcomers playing an active role.

For their part, the newcomers knew little of unions or their reasons for existence. They seldom connected the level of wages and working conditions with the dues they paid or the union card they carried. A series of devices gave the new members—and particularly the black workers—a second-class place in the union.

One black man, Joe James, a shipyard worker with a handsome, ringing baritone voice, organized a committee of fellow shipyard workers to carry their plight to the Cali-

fornia Supreme Court. They complained that they were
confined to an auxiliary union; they were required to pay
dues but were denied the right to vote.

The court's decision called for an "open" union: if a union discriminated in admitting minorities, its right to require
membership as a condition of keeping a job under a closed
shop was contrary to public policy. The auxiliaries disappeared but the underlying discrimination remained a sharp
and troublesome issue for years to come.

In June, 1946, the war ended; shipyards cut back sharply
or closed down. Willie Stokes went to work as a laborer in
a small chemical plant. Now he earned only $6.40 for his
eight hours of work. A year later, like thousands of other
blacks, Stokes was out of work. He had exhausted his unemployment insurance benefits, used up his savings, cashed
his war bonds accumulated in better days. Close to one-third
of the blacks in the Bay Area were unemployed.

They were not alone, but a far greater proportion—
roughly twice as many—were out of work than among white
workers. The discrimination they had suffered in education,
in opportunity, in employment, imposed on them an unemployment rate that, for generations, has remained about
twice as high as the white unemployment rate.

But they still came, crowding into the old ghettos or moving into new ones. There had been 20,000 blacks in the Bay
Area in 1940; there were 120,000 in 1950. San Francisco
itself was home for some 5,000 blacks when the war started,
40,000 ten years later. Only a few San Franciscans, though,
seemed to notice.

20 And now . . .

Today San Francisco sits elegantly on the thumb-tip of her peninsula. Seen from the bay's east shore or the hills of Marin, her buildings stand tall, gray and white and shining in the golden sunlight. Behind them, ribbons of rickrack houses climb the hills. A green spine of coastal mountains supplies a stolid backdrop. Around them the sun and fog stage their always changing light show. The fog stands offshore like a hedgerow of cottony cloud; it may wander among the city's towers, filtering the light into infinitely varied mixtures of silver and gray; or it may blot out the whole city, burying it in dense, dark clouds.

About three-quarters of a million people live on and around these hills. They live in high-rise luxury apartments that now stand where the dilapidated houses of the ghetto poor once stood. On the site of the old and smelly commission market, just beyond the line of Yerba Buena cove, rise the luxurious towers and town houses of Golden Gateway. The land filled for the Panama Pacific International Exposition now accommodates an area of aging, middle-class homes and apartments. Beyond them, to the south and west, lie the stately homes of Pacific Heights, the row houses of Richmond, Parkside, and the Sunset. Scattered among them, and especially in the Mission district, are gentle frame houses, testimony to a time of carpenter skills. Scattered among them, too, are the ghettos: the Fillmore district, Chinatown, the depressing, outworn wartime housing (it was "temporary" twenty-five years ago) of Hunters Point, the inner areas of the Mission district.

Slightly less than half of San Francisco's people in 1960 had at least one foreign parent. Asia was the largest single source; Italy, Germany, Ireland, and the United Kingdom contributed other major national stocks. Even more striking, though, was the rise in the city's nonwhite population. It had been only 5 per cent in 1940. By 1950, it had grown to 10.5 per cent, then to 18.4 per cent in 1960. Nonwhites represented an estimated 22.8 per cent in 1966, and the Spanish-surname population accounted for another 8.8 per cent. Among San Francisco's people, the 1960 census found, were 75,000 Afro-Americans, 36,000 Chinese, 9,500 Japanese, 12,000 Filipinos, 2,000 Koreans, a thousand American Indians.

About half of San Francisco's people work for a living— roughly the same proportion as in 1900. But the shape of the city's economy is quite different. Manufacturing jobs in 1960 represented a far smaller proportion of the city's employment than ever before. Transportation, service, government, finance and insurance, real estate, educational services, hired a far larger proportion of the city's work force. Endless tons of merchandise and raw materials still moved over the city's docks, but she faced growing competition from other ports around the bay. Tourism increasingly represented a major activity. In many ways, though, San Francisco remained the financial headquarters of the West—the forest of towering skyscrapers along Montgomery Street testified to her ruling place in the West's financial world.

The Human Rights Commission reported in 1966 that 18 per cent of the city's white families had incomes below the government-defined boundary of poverty. The proportions of families living in poverty run higher in the city's ghettos. In the Mission district, largely Spanish-speaking, 30 per cent of the families fall below that line. Behind the gloss of Chinatown, San Francisco's major tourist attraction, 41 per cent of the families live in poverty. In Hunters Point, heavily black, 60 per cent of the families are outside the pale. Almost as an invariable rule, unemployment among adult Afro-Americans runs twice as high as among the comparable white group; among black teen-agers it is often four times as high.

With the city's still strong foreign background, the taste and style and customs of the Old World linger, though each day they fade a little. You'll find them in San Francisco's kaleidoscopic choice of restaurants: French and English, German, Armenian, Italian, Chinese (both Mandarin and Cantonese), Japanese, Mexican, Spanish, Swiss, East Indian, Russian, South American, soul food, plain American.

The signs are found, too, in the little grocery stores that offer the seasonings, the vegetables, and the other foods of countless nations. Pasta rollers and kitchen utensils in a North Beach hardware store tell of the Italians that lived there for so many generations. The delicacies of Scandinavia are found not far from the mouth of the Market Street tunnel, Mexican pastries and breads on 16th or 24th Streets. Shops in the Fillmore area or along Third Street echo the accents of the city's black population. The Filipinos gather, to some extent, along Kearny Street. The French are loosely focused around the French Hospital on Geary Boulevard.

The Italian fishermen, long the mainstay of the city's fishing industry, anchor their boats at Fishermen's Wharf. There, both the commercial and the industrial merge in colorful disarray—an Italian area with American streaks and overtones. On the site of old "Japtown" rises a new Japanese center, posh, arty, expensive. Little knots of black-haired youngsters on Chinatown streets in the late afternoon reflect the language schools of their forebears. Traces can still be found of the city's hilltop Russians whose little colony lent color to Potrero Hill.

The city is changing. The slopes of Telegraph Hill, during the great depression, provided cheap housing for unemployed writers and artists, living off great pots of spaghetti and cheap Italian wine. Increasingly fancy and expensive apartment houses drove the old shacks, the makeshift apartments, the basement rooms, from the hills.

The Italian colony that had made its home in North Beach spread slowly into other districts; the new generations moved into larger houses, then on to the suburbs. The small, friendly Italian restaurants along Broadway and Columbus yielded to fancier restaurants and nightclubs and, in recent years, to topless waitresses and naked dancers. In the doorway where an Italian workingman might have stood, picking his teeth after his dinner, come-on barkers make the night hideous.

Upper Grant Avenue once housed little grocery stores specializing in countless styles of Italian pastas. In the fifties a new generation moved into Grant Avenue—the beatniks, they came to be called. Author Jack Kerouac was the Beat Generation's oracle. His philosophy was, "I don't know. I don't care. And it doesn't make any difference." Nonconformity became a way of life, odd styles of dress and beards increasingly frequent. For a time the Beats' life focused on the Coexistence Bagel Shop, hot sun at Aquatic Park, coffee and talk at a coffee house. Then they faded away into respectability. Handcraft artists moved into the little shops scattered among the few remaining Italian grocery stores or restaurants or bars.

Spiritually at least, the Beats' heirs were the hippies who took over the old frame houses around Haight and Ashbury Streets in the late sixties. They, too, sported long hair and beards. Their modes of dress were dredged up from second-hand shops and bargain basements, the Good Will and Salvation Army salvage stores. They held their sometimes defiant "love-ins" and "be-ins," generously spiced with incredibly loud rock bands and sometimes with marijuana, LSD, and other drugs.

The illusions of the "flower children" and their self-proclaimed philosophy of love drew hundreds, probably thousands of youngsters to the new hippie country. On downtown streets they were seen sitting on a busy sidewalk, barefooted, dirty, unkempt. Sometimes they sold "underground" newspapers or panhandled passersby for their "change." Sometimes they merely sat.

Both city and privately-supported medical services found themselves dealing with more and more sick youngsters.

Their physical and emotional illnesses were sometimes complicated by experimenting with, or addiction to, drugs. At other times, they were merely undernourished, unhappily pregnant, or suffering from exposure.

The hippies were the first audience for the "San Francisco Sound," the rock music that swept the country. Groups like the Jefferson Airplane and Country Joe and the Fish and others no less colorfully labeled pounded out an electronically-amplified beat that won attention from the young generation everywhere. They clothed their rebellion against adult values and dominant social mores in high-flown talk of love and freedom. Their sometimes bright, fresh innocence and their special view of life was streaked, sometimes overwhelmed, by somber shades of drugs and sickness. Then they, too, faded away.

The city is changing in other ways. The other San Francisco—the underprivileged minorities, the poor, the outcasts—demands its place in the city's grace. The blacks, the Spanish-speaking, and even the taciturn Chinese are increasingly restive with being denied their equitable part in the city's life.

In the fall of 1963 and the spring of 1964, a series of civil rights demonstrations served startling notice on an often indifferent city. Mass demonstrations picketed supermarkets, then moved on the historic Sheraton Palace Hotel in a massive sit-in. Hundreds were arrested before an agreement on minority hiring could be negotiated. The pattern was repeated again in a demonstration and sit-in focused on motor car dealers. Other sit-downs, marches, strikes, boycotts, and demonstrations testified to minority dissatisfactions.

Targets of anger shifted. At one time it was concentrated on job discrimination, later on segregation, then discrimination in the schools, still later on the invasion of the ghettos by the bulldozers of urban redevelopment. It flared into a bitter and often violent confrontation in the closing weeks of 1968 in a student strike at San Francisco State College under the lead of the Black Students and the Third World Liberation Front, the latter in good part made up of the young people from Spanish-speaking and Mexican families.

The main social problem, the city's Human Rights Commission observed, shifted from remedying today's discrimination to dealing with the results of yesterday's discrimination. The Commission added: "The level of explosive frustration is just as high, if not higher. . . ."

The Commission, along with many other groups and agencies, work at the bits-and-pieces that make up the many problems of employment, training, education, housing, community relations, the built-in patterns of bias and prejudice. Progress often seems slow—even slower as progress itself raises hopes and expectations. The questions become sharper, the answers often seem no more adequate than before. It sometimes sounds as if everybody is talking at once and nobody is listening. The tone and temper of the voices rise. Conflict echoes along the streets of the city.

San Francisco is not alone among American cities, perhaps not even unique, in the problems she faces. She is tortured by occasional smog, the product of too many cars going too many places at once, and the promise of more to come. Traffic grows heavier; new, swooping freeways become overcrowded, obsolescent almost from the moment they are opened. San Francisco finally drew a line—no more freeways.

The city builds a rapid transit system, accompanied by stentorian arguments, quarrels over money, disputes over design. She sometimes raids her neighbors, ignores them or seeks to dictate to them, when the need for regional developments, regional collaboration, seems increasingly apparent every day. Too frequently she seems to be dragged on by developments, rather than planning and implementing her own future.

The city often seems ill-prepared and often unwilling to deal with infinite problems of poverty and race, with decent housing at a price most of her citizens can pay, with open and freely moving traffic, with clean air and unpolluted water. She is often indifferent to the landmarks of her past, replacing them at times with dullness and monotony and cheap tinsel. She displays great tolerance for strange, weird, and unpopular voices, only to turn sharply and viciously at times on some protestant or demonstrator. She blends inequities rooted in race with yearning for good things. She mixes measures of democracy with resentment of change.

The other San Francisco is forcing a confrontation with many of these unpleasant aspects of the city's life. With increasing vigor it calls on the city and her people to practice what they have preached these many years—the tolerance, the understanding, the cosmopolitanism, the boldness and creativeness that have always been her special claim. The process is almost always noisy and often painful, but it's also healthful and vital.

Beyond the clamor is the future.

Some thoughts on further reading

Library shelves are sway-backed with books about San Francisco, the Gold Rush, the fire and earthquake. The city inevitably figures prominently in the countless attempts to tell the history of California or to define the Golden State's place in history.

Much of it, of course, is dry and dusty. Much of it is badly written, hard to chew and difficult to digest. But there is also a good deal of well-written history, informative as well as entertaining. The explorer, though, should be warned that the diet is poorly balanced. Myth and sentiment often get in the way of a realistic, gritty feel of the city's past.

History tends to lean heavily on the Gold Rush and the Forty-niners, the silver millionaires, the railroad kings. The fire and earthquake come in for a good deal of attention, too. But sometimes I get the impression that the history of the city seems to have stopped about 1906. Or, at best, when the bay bridges were built in the thirties. The story of workingmen and their unions and their struggle for recognition gets scant attention. The abuse of the Chinese in the 70's and 80's can hardly be escaped, but it is not often seen as part of a thread that persists from the city's beginnings to the present day. The place of minorities seems, in much of the writing, to have been to lend color and quaintness. Only occasionally does the reader realize that skins were yellow and black and red as well as white.

The tragic evacuation of the Japanese during World War II has not, to my knowledge, been adequately reported. Nor has the influx of the city's now sizable black population. Nor the city's response to its unending flood of immigrants of every kind.

Such broad and sweeping generalizations are not invariably applicable in whole, all the time, in every case. However, they are true enough, I think, to serve as a necessary caution in approaching the city's history. Having sounded this warning, let me suggest a few (of very many) ways of getting deeper into San Francisco's past.

Fiction is often a painless way to start. Gertrude Atherton and Bret Harte, among others, have both told of the courtship of Rezanov and the lovely Concepcion Arguello. Harte romanticized the miner's flannel shirt and dirty boots in his fascinating stories, "The Outcasts of Poker Flat," "The Luck of Roaring Camp," and many more. Helen Hunt Jackson in *Ramona* reflected the plight of the Indian. Frank Norris effectively reflects other facets of California life in *McTeague* and *The Octopus*. William Saroyan caught the feel of the depression years in San Francisco in some of his early writings.

On the nonfiction shelves, the entries are endless. For my part, I found Harold Gilliam's *San Francisco Bay* exceptionally well done. *This Is San Francisco* is a delight; how fact and legend assay, though, I can't say. I liked Miriam Allen DeFord's *They Were San Franciscans,* biographical sketches of a number of not too well-known old-timers. I thought Monica Sutherland's *The Damnedest Finest Ruins* an effective story of the earthquake. If only to thumb through it, the reader ought to try to find *Pictures of Old Chinatown* by Arnold Genthe with text by Will Irwin. These pre-fire photos of the Chinese in San Francisco, though somewhat glossy and romanticized, still provide a unique view of another day. There are, of course, many, many more, each leading to several others. The interested reader will happily unravel the chain.

In more specialized fields, the reader might want to look into *Frame-up* by Curt Gentry, a detailed study of the Mooney case. Professor Ira B. Cross wrote the definitive history of labor in California, but it ends with the 1901 water-front strike. I have written a short history of California labor, *Sky Full of Storm,* that I recommend. Jack D. Forbes sketched the Afro-American past in *Afro-Americans in the Far West.*

These suggestions are by no means intended to be definitive, but merely some places to start. Happy hunting.

Index